THE CLOUD OF UNKNOWING
Reflections on Selected Texts

AUSTIN COOPER OMI

THE CLOUD OF UNKNOWING

Reflections on Selected Texts

Burns & Oates

Published in Great Britain 1991
by Burns & Oates Limited
Wellwood, North Farm Road, Tunbridge Wells, Kent TN2 3DR

First published in 1989
by St Paul Publications, Homebush, Australia

Copyright © Austin Cooper OMI, 1989

ISBN (UK) 0 86012 188 7

All rights reserved. No part of this book may be reproduced in any form, by print, photoprint, microfilm, microfiche, mechanical recording, photocopying, translation, or any other means, known or as yet unknown, or stored in an information retrieval system, without written permission obtained beforehand from Burns & Oates Ltd.

Printed and bound in Great Britain by
Biddles Ltd, Guildford and King's Lynn

Contents

Introduction	7
Part I	
Your Life is Hid with Christ in God	13
1. Come Holy Spirit	15
2. In Christ Jesus	21
3. To the Fullness of Truth and Life	28
4. In the Fullness of Time	34
5. In the Church	39
6. Growth in God	45
7. The Best Part	53
8. Desiring God	60
Part II	
Be Still and Know that I Am God	71
9. On the Mountain	73
10. The Cloud	80
11. Loving Presence	89
12. The Word	98
13. Forgetting	106
14. Re-membering	116
15. Growth	121
Part III	
You Will Know Them by Their Fruits	133
16. Bearing Fruit	135
17. Christian Maturity	144
18. Freedom	153
19. Love	164
20. Transfiguration	174

Introduction

The aim of this book is threefold. In the first instance it seeks to introduce the reader to the English works of the anonymous, 14th century author who wrote the *The Cloud of Unknowing* and several other, smaller and lesser known works. These works, all dealing with contemplative prayer, are:

> *The Cloud of Unknowing:* the best known of these works and also the longest. It contains many affective sections, and repays slow, meditative reading.
>
> *The Book of Privy Counsel:* a later work answering some of the problems that arose from a reading of *The Cloud*; it is a shorter, much more tightly organised work.
>
> *The Epistle of Prayer:* a very compact treatment of contemplative prayer. Perhaps the literary gem of this author.
>
> *Denis Hid Divinity:* a translation of the work of an Eastern writer known as the Pseudo-Dionysius (c 500). It teaches the approach to God as the great mystery.
>
> *A Treatise on the Discernment of Spirits:* is not an original work either, being a free adaptation of two sermons by St Bernard (1090-1153).
>
> *Benjamin* or *A Treatise on the Study of Wisdom that Men Call Benjamin:* is also a free adaptation of an earlier work by Richard, a Scot who was a monk at St Victor's (d 1173). Probably the earliest work of our author.
>
> *A Letter on the Discernment of Stirrings:* seeks to clarify the way a committed Christian should make practical judgments.

The Cloud enjoyed some measure of popularity before the Reformation, judging by the number of manuscripts extant; and it was known to English Catholics in the following centuries, having been commented upon by the famous Benedictine monk, Austin Baker (1575-1641), who did so much to keep alive an interest in medieval Catholic spirituality. However it was not printed until as late as 1871, and not made available in a modernised English version until that published by Evelyn Underhill in 1912.

This century has witnessed a growing popularity for this work, and it has undergone several fresh renditions since the pioneering work of Evelyn Underhill. It is almost as though it was written for our age.

The Cloud teaches a form of prayer known as 'contemplation' in which the person does not use words or images but simply acts of the will, desiring or 'wanting' God. Such prayer has often aroused fears of a certain imbalance: it seemed to place too great an emphasis on the work done by God — grace; while at the same time it seemed that the human being was overly passive. These fears reached their zenith in 17th century France with the condemnation of writers known as 'Quietists'. However it is agreed that the author of *The Cloud* is certainly not guilty of any excesses in this regard. Indeed he loves to speak of 'the work' of contemplation; the human being is certainly not inactive, let alone entirely passive.

Borrowing heavily from the Pseudo-Dionysius, our author teaches the 'negative' approach to God; that is, we 'know' God as a mystery beyond all our words and images. Yet he also employs a host of images to impart his teaching. He speaks of a crown, a tree bearing fruit, a marriage and so on. All these images will be found in the pages of scripture. Indeed he draws on the Bible a great deal and delights in the Martha-Mary story, and makes use of figures such as Moses. But his most characteristic image is the 'cloud'. In the last analysis we stand before God as before an enveloping mystery who is 'beyond' clear images and who is beyond sight; yet this cloud shrouds a presence which is creative, healing and loving.

So compellingly attractive is this mysterious presence that anyone seeking it will struggle to place a 'cloud of forgetting' over all else. Here we are in the midst of a deeply personal experience; yet it takes place within a clearly defined context: it requires a commitment to Christ and the Church. In no way does this teaching imply a rejection of the body of Christ which was so sorely tried and distracted in the author's day. Indeed contemplation enriches Church and society for the contemplative must necessarily show forth the fruit of contemplation — love. Being more deeply committed to the mystery of God, one becomes more finely attuned to one's fellow humans.

As well as illustrating and commenting on such teachings, it is also hoped that this book will show how they relate very easily to both the wider Catholic tradition and also to the spiritual needs of contemporary Christians. The author was very sensitive to the possibility of his being misunderstood, and indeed it seems that he was misrepresented and criticised. But what he taught has a clear affinity to the great spiritual tradition of the Christian East. His debt to the Pseudo-Dionysius is one clear indication of that; but his spiritual ancestry must surely include St Gregory of Nyssa (332-395) whose *Life of Moses* predates much of his teaching; and indeed we can link him with the 'Desert Fathers' and their stress on spiritual direction. And in the Western tradition he has an obvious love for St Augustine (354-430); St Gregory the Great (540-604) as well as others of a later date such as St Bernard and Richard of St Victor as noted above.

Our author is also one of a cluster of brilliant spiritual writers of 14th century England such as Richard Rolle, Julian of Norwich and Walter Hilton. *The Ladder of*

Perfection by Hilton was written after *The Cloud*, but the two works have so many similarities that some scholars thought Hilton to have been the author of *The Cloud*. This theory is no longer propagated, but the similarities show that both authors drew from a common heritage. Not only does the author relate easily to many predecessors and contemporaries but he also finds an echo in much that has been written since his time, and in many ways predates much of the teaching of St John of the Cross (1542-1591). But whatever similarities he might display with those from whom he might have learnt, and from whom he doubtless borrowed, he always manages to display a unique personality and distinctive style.

It remains true, of course, that an author is always a child of his or her own age. *The Cloud* and its satellites date from an age which was witnessing the breakdown of much of the medieval synthesis: these works are not written in the highly structured and economic style associated with an Aquinas or a Bonaventure; nor were they written in Latin. Yet the vernacular in which they were written displays something of the great vigour and vitality that were signs of hope in an age of dislocation and decay. For this author lived in an age which witnessed the tedious and disruptive Hundred Years War between England and France; the Great Western Schism had introduced Western Christians to the harrowing reality of a divided Christendom; society suffered serious dislocation as a result of the Peasants' Revolt of 1381; and perhaps most pervasive and enduring of all was the frightening uncertainty which came in the wake of the Black Death. Yet our author never allows any of this to colour his outlook or drive him to extreme positions. Throughout he retains a down-to-earth realism coupled with flashes of good humour.

Although we do not know the dates of his birth or death, the language he employed has enabled the most prominent of *The Cloud* scholars, Dr Phyllis Hodgson, to conclude that the work 'was written in the northern part of the central East Midlands' (*The Cloud of Unknowing* p 1). While no details of his life are known for sure, his writings contain many pointers to his having been a priest, and many scholars think he was a Cistercian or (more probably) a Carthusian monk. While *The Cloud* was written in the first instance for one person, the author might well have had a wider audience in mind; his works represent a splendid example of pastoral care in the form of spiritual direction.

Although his age and ours might have some similarities, we do not need to seek them too diligently. For this cluster of writings represents a 'timeless' aspect of our tradition of spirituality; it is partly that which marks these works out as classics. They certainly can speak to men and women of this age. Indeed one of the most hopeful signs of vitality in the contemporary world is the increased yearning for a deeper prayer life. It is hoped that this book will offer some encouragement to those engaged in such a quest.

Finally, it is hoped that this commentary will jog readers into reading the texts themselves. In the end nothing can take the place of a return to the sources; the effort involved will certainly prove well worth the cost.

As this book is offered as a devotional and reflective commentary rather than a scholarly one, footnotes and references have been kept to a minimum. The following short bibliography might prove some help to those who wish to read either the texts themselves or more learned commentaries:

Phyllis Hodgson (ed.), *The Cloud of Unknowing and the Book Privy Counselling* (Early English Text Society, London: Oxford University Press, 1944).

Phyllis Hodgson (ed.), *Deonise Hid Divinite and Other Treatises on contemplative prayer related to the Cloud of*

Unknowing (Early English Text Society, London: Oxford University Press, 1958). (The translations in this commentary have been made from these two works.)

Evelyn Underhill (ed.), *The Book of Contemplation the which is called The Cloud of Unknowing in which a soul is oned with God* (London: Stuart and Watkins, 1970) is an almost literal rendering of the original and captures much of the vigour and colour of the author's language.

James Walsh S.J., (ed.), *The Cloud of Unknowing* (NY, Paulist, 1981) and *The Pursuit of Wisdom* (NY, Paulist, 1988); these two volumes in the Classics of Western Spirituality series provide a modern English version of all the works with lengthy scholarly introduction and notes.

Clifton Wolters (ed.), *The Cloud of Unknowing and Other Works* (Harmondsworth: Penguin Books, 1978); and also Clifton Wolters (ed.), *A Study of Wisdom. Three Tracts by the Author of the Cloud of Unknowing* (Fairacres, Oxford: SLG Press, 1980). These two publications contain all the English works by the author of *The Cloud*, and are in eminently readable prose.

Two commentaries of some interest are: Johnston, *The Mysticism of the Cloud of Unknowing* (Wheathampstead: Anthony Clarke, 1978); and Constantino S. Nieva, *This Transcending God* (London: The Mitre Press, 1971).

Special thanks are due to the members of the community at St Mary's for enabling this book to be written (and especially to Eric Alleaume OMI for his unfailing patience with word-processor problems). To these, and to all whom the author has encouraged to respond to the grace of prayer, this book is warmly dedicated.

Austin Cooper, OMI
St Mary's
Mulgrave, Victoria, Australia

Part 1
Your Life is Hid with Christ in God (Col 3:3)

1. Come Holy Spirit

*God
to you all hearts are open
and to you every will speaks
and from you no secret is hidden.
I beseech you,
so to cleanse the intentions of my heart
with the unspeakable gift of your grace
that I may perfectly love you
and worthily praise you*
(The Cloud, *Prayer before the Preface).*

Although this book, *The Cloud of Unknowing,* treats of a deeply personal form of prayer, the author begins with a collect, or prayer, from the public worship of the Church. The above prayer, placed before the Prologue of *The Cloud,* is from the Roman liturgy and is found in the Mass seeking the grace of the Holy Spirit. It dates from the 8th century and is attributed to Alcuin of York, the monk scholar at the court of the emperor Charlemagne. It still has a place in the Roman Liturgy. It was also selected by Archbishop Cranmer as the opening prayer (following the Lord's Prayer) in the Communion Service of the 1549 *Book of Common Prayer,* and is retained in revised Anglican liturgies. Hence it is well known to a wide range of contemporary Christians.

By placing this prayer at the beginning of the work, the author reminds us that even the most personal of our prayers can, and at times should, draw on the treasures of the liturgy; and that even the most individual aspects of our Christian life are experienced as part of a larger 'body'. We are never alone, and certainly we are not alone when we turn to God in prayer. Indeed our very turning to him is a response to one who is present; who invites us to pray; who enables us to do so; and who empowers us to address God as Father.

So prayer begins with the Holy Spirit; indeed it is the Spirit who prays in us for

> the Spirit helps us in our weakness; for we do not know how to pray as we ought, but the Spirit himself intercedes for us with sighs too deep for words *(Rom 8:26).*

To be committed to prayer is to be in touch with the great Pentecostal event. And that event was both ecclesial and deeply personal: the disciples were 'all together in one place' yet the tongues of fire were 'distributed and resting on each one of them' (Acts 2:1-3). What was a gift for all was also a gift for each one individually. And in the wake of that great event the 'multitude came together': there was a group, a body of people with some unity; yet 'each one heard (the disciples) speaking in his own language' (Acts 2:6).

It is well for us to remember that our first personal encounter with the mystery of Pentecost was at Baptism. On that occasion we were breathed on by the breath of God and made members of a body, the Church; yet we were also confirmed in our individuality and given a name. As God knew Moses 'by name' (Ex 32:12) and the Lord, the good shepherd, 'calls his own sheep by name' (Jn 10:3), so each one of us has an individuality recognised and sealed by the Spirit. Here, in the ecclesial event of Baptism, the Spirit comes to both the whole Church and also to the individual. The strange mixture of the communal and the individual means that the person is not like one of several peas in a pod; being Christian does not mean having a colourless anonymity. Nor on the other hand does it mean an aggressive self assertiveness. The grace of individuality is also the gift of peace and harmony. Our individual gifts are essentially related to others; they are given for mutual up-building. St Paul was conscious of this when he reminded his Christians at Corinth of the need for harmony between the personal and the communal:

> by one Spirit are all baptised into one body — Jews or Greeks, slaves or free — and all were made to drink of one Spirit *(1 Cor 12:13)*.

And along with this unity in the Spirit, went that sometimes bewildering and always colourful variety of gifts:

> there is a variety of gifts, but the same Spirit; and there are varieties of service but the same Lord; and there are varieties of working but it is the same Lord who inspires them all in everyone. To each is given the manifestation of the Spirit for the common good *(1 Cor 12:4-7)*.

So at the very beginning of our journey with this author, he prompts us to remember our deeply personal commitment to prayer and our own individual gift of the Spirit of God. And at the same time he reminds us that this gift is not given in isolation but comes to us in the undying power of Pentecost.

As is customary with collects from the Roman liturgy, this prayer which the author places at the head of his work begins with a profession of faith. We profess our belief in the God who knows all hearts, who is aware of all the desires in the human heart, and from whom there is no secret: the Spirit searches everything, even the depths of God (1 Cor 2:10). The Spirit who knows the deepest longings of the human heart, even better than we know ourselves, helps us to appreciate something of these longings:

> We have received not the spirit of the world, but the Spirit which is from God, that we might understand the gifts

bestowed on us by God. And we impart this in words not taught by human wisdom but taught by the Spirit, interpreting spiritual truths to those who possess the Spirit *(1 Cor 2:12-13)*.

As we walk our Christian way we need to pause and recall that we are steeped in mystery; we carry with us a presence of God given us at Baptism; we can be willing instruments in bringing this mystery to the world. Yet we are dealing with a gift about which we know so little, and only have hints and suggestions. The Lord is the only one who really knows us. He alone searches the mind (Jer 17:10) with complete thoroughness. The psalmist recognises this basic truth of God knowing us when he prays:

> O Lord you search me and you know me,
> you know my resting and my rising,
> you discern my purpose from afar.
> You mark when I walk or lie down,
> all my ways are open to you.
> Before ever a word is on my tongue
> you know it O Lord, through and through.
> Behind and before you beseige me,
> your hand ever laid upon me.
> Too wonderful for me this knowledge,
> too high, beyond my reach
> *(Ps 138[139]:1-6)*.

We could profitably reflect upon this psalm at some leisure. When we come to prayer, we leave ourselves open to the all-knowing and all searching gaze of God. We are 'known' in ways and in depths that we cannot know ourselves. We stand before the 'God who knows the secrets of the heart' (Ps 44:21). God knows us better than we can ever know ourselves.

But God does not know us in some detached, intellectual fashion, as we might be said to know some object or fact outside ourselves. Psalm 138 also hints that we are 'in God' somewhat after the fashion of being in a womb; we might seek to escape, rushing off to distant mountains or to the depths of the earth or across the distant seas but 'you are there ... your right hand would hold me fast'. One cannot hide in the dark for

> even darkness is not dark for you
> and the night is as clear as the day.
> For it was you who created my being,
> knit me together in my mother's womb.
> O search me God and know my heart.
> O test me and know my thoughts.
> See that I follow not the wrong path
> and lead me in the path of life eternal
> *(Ps 138[139]:10-13,23-24).*

So the knowledge which God has of the human heart is a loving, creative and healing knowledge. Thus the second part of the opening prayer moves on from the statement of belief in this all-knowing and all-loving God, to make an appropriate petition. We ask that he would cleanse the intentions of our heart so that we might perfectly love him and worthily praise him. So we pray for purity of heart. This alone enables us to experience God (Mt 5:8).

In the prayer taught by the author of *The Cloud*, we combine two aspects of our spirituality. It is an ecclesial thing, for we have been introduced into the faith and nurtured in it by others. So we take our cue from a great liturgical prayer. But this author is also deeply aware that our spirituality is profoundly personal. And in our most personal and individual stance, we leave ourselves totally open, receptive and pliable: we ask that we might be 'known' in the sense of being cleansed of evil; made perfectly lovable; and so enabled to give fitting service to the God who requires that we praise him in spirit and in truth (Jn 4:24).

But a personal aspect of our spirituality is never simply that: it always has its communal ramifications. The gift of the Spirit to the individual is a gift which in some way also enriches the whole body of Christians and also the whole world. The Spirit will endow the individual with attitudes which make for a better world. At the very least the person of prayer will be less hasty in making judgments about others. And there is also the possibility that the Spirit will give an individual a special ministry to 'correct' others. While clearly such a gift is not to be lightly presumed, when it *is* given it would be truly prophetic. It would also be given in 'perfect love'. And it would complement and not negate properly established authority. In one short chapter of *The Cloud*, the author harmonises all these communal and individual strands:

> By whom shall human actions be judged? Surely by those who have authority and pastoral care which is either given publicly by the laws and ordinance of Holy Church, or else privately in a special movement of the Holy Spirit in perfect love. But everyone should beware and not presume to blame or condemn the faults of others, unless he feels truly moved to this work by the Holy Spirit; otherwise such a person might very well be completely mistaken. So beware! Judge yourself if you wish, by yourself, your God and your spiritual father. Leave others alone *(The Cloud 30)*.

There, one has the picture of a balanced individual: quite at home with the demands of his particular calling; and also quite attuned to life in a corporate body. The Spirit who comes to the individual at prayer, is a truly creative presence.

2. In Christ Jesus

> *In the name of the Father*
> *and of the Son*
> *and of the Holy Spirit.*
> *I charge and implore you, with all the power and strength that love can command: you should not write or speak (of this matter) to anyone unless that person has decided firmly and sincerely to follow Christ perfectly* (The Cloud, *Prologue*).

Having invoked the Holy Spirit the author proceeds to address us in the name of the most blessed Trinity. The Spirit empowers us to enter the life of God: Father, Son and Holy Spirit. As St Irenaeus (d 200) so succinctly expressed it:

> The Spirit prepares man for the Son of God, the Son brings him to the Father, and the Father bestows on him incorruptibility for eternal life, which comes to everyone from his beholding God
> (Irenaeus, *Against Heresies, IV, 20*).

Thus 'beholding God' is a grace which is bestowed by the coming of the Spirit. It is the Spirit who gives life. Although our author has firmly placed his instruction under the guidance of the Holy Spirit and within the context of our life in the Blessed Trinity, he is fearful of being misunderstood. These fears are to be often repeated in the Prologue and elsewhere. Indeed the prayer of which he speaks can all too easily be misrepresented as daydreaming, time-wasting or self-deception. The existence of some tension, however, is not to be wondered at: the strange harmony between the deepest individual aspects of our spirituality and its ecclesial, communal aspects are often not easily reconciled. Indeed some pain and misunderstanding are essential ingredients of growth. None of us can grow without experiencing the tension between our individuality and the responsibilities involved in belonging to society.

But our author is very clear. If we are to grow it must be within and through the mystery of Christ. The starting point for this type of prayer is a deep commitment to Jesus Christ. This is the first of three conditions which he posits as prerequisites for contemplative prayer. He sees it as utterly essential.

What does such a commitment mean to us today? When we read the gospels we are confronted with the challenging question: 'who do people say that I am?' What, indeed, is being said about Jesus? What are people saying to us concerning the Lord? Many people are 'saying' something about him by their explicit or implicit rejection of him. To be committed to Christ in this century is to be committed to someone who is seen as irrelevant; and to be committed to a Christian mysticism is tantamount to opting for something that many will regard as a sheer waste of time and opportunity. Indeed to be Christian today is to be in some real sense 'marginalised'; to be unfashionable; and in some instances to be dangerously radical. So the gospel question 'who do people say that I am?' can have some value in challenging us to articulate our own commitment to Jesus Christ. Much that is being said might be wholesome; some of it might be challenging and surprising; somewhere there will be hints and pointers to the truth. But all too many people find it easy to talk 'about' the Christian faith. We are challenged to do more than that by the second question: 'who do *you* say that I am?' Our faith cannot be merely an interesting romp among opinions or an intellectual dabbling in theories. Each one of us has to make a decision, and deepen our commitment to Jesus as Lord.

This is not an easy matter nor a mere adoption of a theory. When we read the gospels we find varying responses to Jesus that cannot be merely relegated to the pages of history. Each one of them suggests a surprisingly contemporary challenge, each one of them gives us a real indicator for Christian practice. For instance, there were some who rejected Jesus because he was all too familiar to them:

> Is not this the carpenter's son?
> Is not his mother called Mary?
> And are not his brethren James and Joseph and Simon and Judas?
> Are not all his sisters with us?
> Where then did this man get all this?
> *(Mt 13:55-56).*

So the one who was so close and familiar was rejected. To be committed to Jesus Christ involves accepting the ordinary and commonplace; it's all too easy for us to miss the significance of such things; to fail to see that our God is a God who is 'so near' to us (Deut 4:7); that he comes in the most unexpected and seemingly insignificant ways.

There is a profound Christian wisdom in being able to appreciate something of the mystery of God in the simple things of life. That was the enduring charm of the wise men from the east; not finding the expected one in the courts of the great they were prepared to lay their gifts and their hearts before a helpless and seemingly insignificant little child. We who are so deeply conditioned by attitudes stemming from the Enlightenment period need to foster what Karl Rahner has called 'everyday mysticism' and not reduce the familiar and the ordinary to the level of trivia or merely physical phenomena. Rather we must see them as an invitation and an opening to the eternal.

To be committed to Jesus Christ challenges us to recognise the mystery of God thinly veiled by what is close at hand and seemingly commonplace: to follow Jesus Christ is to be open to the deepest possibilities of *this* time and *this* place.

Others, of course, rejected Jesus because he could be dismissed as one in league with evil:

> Behold a glutton and a drunkard, friend of tax collectors and sinners *(Mt 11:19)*.

And the Pharisees, hearing of the works of Jesus proclaimed:

> It is only by Beelzebul, the prince of demons, that this man casts out demons *(Mt 12:24)*.

It is so easy to take a 'holier-than-thou' attitude to religion; to want a faith so 'spiritual' that it does not touch the warp and woof of everyday living. Such is not the way of Jesus Christ. He came to save the world; to transfigure it into the Kingdom of God, and it always spoke to him of the beauty of that Kingdom. He used this world as his 'teaching-aid' and made us see a deeper meaning to mustard seeds, fish in a net, birds in the air and seed scattered. He also used it as his instrument to bring healing. On one occasion he even used mud and spittle, which must have horrified the more 'spiritual' among his audience. And now bread and wine, and water and oil, are among the ordinary and simple things that form an ongoing part of the process. So the one committed to Jesus Christ does not despise the 'world' but seeks to redeem it, to appreciate its potentiality for good and be open to flashes of God-light entering by surprising windows.

Still others wanted to see Jesus as a wonder-worker. The quest 'Teacher we wish to see a sign from you' (Mt 12:38) and the jibe 'Prophesy to us ... who is it that struck you' (Mt 26:68) hardly indicated a genuine search for wisdom. Sometimes we can fall into the trap of seeking the bizarre and the unusual. Yet if our hearts are really open, we can be touched by the Spirit of Jesus in the everyday tasks of life and in the simplicity of sacrament.

And the gospels present us with moments of great enthusiasm for Jesus: what a 'heady' experience we meet in the euphoria of that first 'Palm Sunday'. Yet the enthusiastic admirers and supporters soon turned into an angry mob shouting 'crucify him, crucify him'. Obviously a commitment to Christ involves some consistency; we cannot oscillate between emotional support and angry rejection. But we can all too easily do something close enough to that in practice. Perhaps for most of our lives our 'fidelity' and 'constancy' might mean only (or predominantly) a constant and faithful turning back to Christ after our moments of indifference, foolishness and sin. To follow Christ means to accept a 'death' to sin and a being alive to a new life which comes to us in the guise of mercy. The death and the resurrection do not take place once and for all, but are a process involving a series of fresh beginnings after humbling mistakes.

So the one who 'follows Christ perfectly', as our author insists, is the person who is prepared to struggle with the challenge to lose life in order to gain it (Mk 8:36); and who is prepared to 'decrease'; to accept the simple and ordinary things of life in order that we might find that Jesus Christ 'increases' (Jn 3:30) in ways we never imagined possible; and one who is willing to take up a cross and follow the path of Christ (Mt 16:24). Our author makes this very explicit:

> This is the true condition of the perfect lover: he completely and utterly strips himself of himself for the sake of the one he loves and he will not suffer himself to be clothed in anything other than the one he loves
> *(Privy Counsel 8).*

This is to 'put on' the Lord Jesus Christ as Paul would have us do (Rom 13-14 and Gal 3:27). And this is to answer the Lord's second question (who do *you* say that I am?) and assert with St Peter: 'You are the Christ' (Mk 8:27). Christ is the truth about God and the way to God. For the Christian there can be no other 'mysticism', there is no other way to enter into the mystery of God:

> No one has ever seen God, but the only Son who dwells in the bosom of the Father has made him known to us *(Jn 1:18)*.

Nonetheless when our author tells us that we must be willing to 'follow Christ perfectly' we might be complacent enough to imagine that we *already* 'know' Christ; that we are familiar with what the Church teaches about him, and that we are close to him in prayer and sacrament. It is no harm to remind ourselves of the way Jesus had to chide Philip:

> Have you been with me so long and yet you do not know me Philip? *(Jn 14:9)*.

We can always deepen our appreciation of Jesus Christ and our commitment to him. Such, indeed, is the whole point of the author's teaching. Christ is the only way by which we might pierce the veil and enter into deeper contact with the divine:

> It is a marvellous household, this life of the Spirit, for our Lord is not only the doorkeeper, he is also the Doorway: he is the former by his divinity and the latter by his humanity. He tells us so in the gospels, (Jn 10:9 and Jn 10:1) ... I have made myself available. I am the door by reason of my manhood. He who enters by me will be safe *(Privy Counsel 9)*.

And this entry through Jesus Christ means a deep personal union with God:

Christ's sacrifice was made for all men and not just for some individuals in particular. Thus he truly and perfectly sacrifices himself for the good of all. He does all that is possible to knit all men to God as effectively as he himself is *(Privy Counsel 3)*.

By his very nature Christ wishes to give us this gift of 'union' with God:

> There is a power in love that enables it to share everything. So love Jesus and everything that he has is yours *(The Cloud 4)*.

So to be committed to Jesus Christ means grasping the opportunities offered 'here and now'. The love of God is touching us through ordinary things. We need to recapture something of the insight of William Blake:

> Everything that lives is Holy.
>
> If the doors of perception were cleansed, everything would appear to man as it is, infinite
> *(America* and *The Marriage of Heaven and Hell)*.

3. To the Fullness of Truth and Life

> *(Secondly) you should not write or speak (of this matter) to anyone unless that person has already determined to follow Christ perfectly, not only in active living but also to the highest point of contemplative living possible by grace in this present life* (The Cloud, *Prologue*).

Writing as a Medievalist, the author quite possibly had in mind those called to live a 'contemplative life' in a religious order. Such an assumption would be reasonable for an author in those days. But it is not difficult to see that his words can have a much wider application. The call to 'contemplation' cannot be simply limited to a select few. Indeed his own words quoted above would seem to imply that the grace of contemplation is one that is an understandable growth from our basic commitment to Christ. Commentators differ as to whether in fact our author intended any such 'liberal' view: William Johnston SJ holds that he did take such a wide view, while Constantino Sarmiento Nieva takes the opposing view. Without entering into that dispute we can be content with what seems to be a reasonable interpretation of the author's teaching. As we have seen, a commitment to Christ is the basic thing.

In a very graphic and earthy manner, he speaks of the healing touch of Jesus Christ:

> Take the good gracious God just as he is, and simply lay him on your sick self just as you are. Or to put it in another way, lift up your sick self, just as you are, and

endeavour to touch by your desire the good and gracious God just as he is. Touching him is an endless help as we see from the evidence of the gospel: 'If I touch even his garments, I shall be made well' (Mk 5:28 and Lk 8:44) *(Privy Counsel 2)*.

Time and again our author prompts us to begin with the stark facts. He is an utter realist. We must take ourselves 'just as we are', no illusions, no pretensions, no excuses — just the unadorned self. This realistic acceptance of self is a very significant aspect of the author's teaching and we must return to it later.

In a manner we can describe as typically medieval, he then divides the Christian life into two: active and contemplative, the latter being 'higher' than the former. And each of these is similarly divided into two parts, a higher and a lower.

> These two lives are so coupled together that although they differ in some respects, neither of them can be had fully without some part of the other ... One may not be fully active, without being in some way contemplative, nor fully contemplative (at least here on earth) without being partly active *(The Cloud 8)*.

This life in Christ, then, is envisaged as something like a ladder with several rungs (a favourite image of spiritual writers). Indeed there is good reason to think that the little treatise entitled a *Ladder of Foure Ronges* was also written by *The Cloud* author. The point of such images is, of course, that our life in Christ must grow, it cannot be static. Belief in Christ does not simply involve making a basic credal profession; it is a life that must be lived and life implies growth and development.

For all his 'earthy' language and his typically medieval love of hierarchy, our author is very careful not to be trapped in his own language. When he speaks of Christ's ascension and our ascending he is merely using a manner of speech. Likewise when he speaks of the Holy Spirit 'coming down' it is merely a matter of linguistic suitability, of what is 'seemly':

> Apart from this seemliness, he needed no more to have gone upwards than downwards ... For heaven is as much down as up, and up as down, behind as before, before as behind and on one side as on the other. For whoever has a true desire to be in heaven, then at the same time he is spiritually there *(The Cloud 60).*

He is concerned all along with the person who has a deep commitment to Christ and who would wish to walk in his pathway and share in his life. Such a follower must have a real and genuine desire for heaven, that is, to be with God. A commitment to Christ means that in some real and spiritual way, heaven is already a fact. In looking at this following of Christ as a growth or ascent up a ladder, our author makes much of the story of Mary and Martha, taking Mary to be identical with Magdalen. Mary is typical of sinners called to a life of contemplation *(The Cloud 16 and 22).* In treating of this story he gives some flesh and colour to his description of the Christian life as a fourfold 'ascent' *(The Cloud 8).* Martha is very busy about many things, and that was 'full good and holy for it is the first part of the active life' *(The Cloud 17).* The second part of the active life and the first part of the contemplative life merge together, and he describes this as considering

> the preciousness of his blessed body, and the sweet voice and words of his manhood *(The Cloud 17).*

This presumably could be an 'active' or external preoccupation with Jesus, or a deeper and spiritual appreciation of his character and the meaning of his words. He then continues to describe very simply what captivated Mary and held her undivided attention to the exclusion of all else:

> She beheld with all the love of her heart the most sovereign wisdom of his Godhead shrouded in the deep words of his manhood *(The Cloud 17)*.

What Mary had begun here in this scene was to have its completion in heaven:

> Mary had chosen the best part which shall not be taken away from her. Because the perfect stirring of love which begins here in this life, is the same as that which shall last for ever in the bliss of heaven *(The Cloud 20)*.

This 'ascent' of Mary from what he considered a state of habitual sin through conversion to the heights of contemplation has been made possible by the whole mystery of Christ. And indeed he sees the latter stages as simply a share in the grace of the ascension:

> If it had been that there was no higher perfection in this life than to contemplate him in his humanity, I believe that he would not have ascended to heaven while this world still lasted, nor would we have withdrawn his bodily presence from his special lovers on earth. But there is a higher perfection which a person may reach in this life, namely, a purely spiritual experience of the love of his Godhead *(Privy Counsel 9)*.

And in support of this teaching he quotes the gospel: 'It is to your advantage that I go away' (Jn 16:7) and also St Augustine 'If his human form is not withdrawn from our sight, we shall not be able spiritually to gaze upon the love of his Godhead' *(Sermon 143)*. Thus we do not simply abide in a 'physical' or superficial human knowledge of Jesus; we are also empowered by grace to enter the mystery of Christ. We can pass beyond what is 'seen' to what is 'unseen', that is to the mystery of God. So St Teresa assures us that some Christians can 'see' what is beyond human sight:

> I saw Christ close by me, or, to speak more correctly, felt Him; for I saw nothing with the eyes of the body, nothing with the eyes of the soul ... (St Teresa *Life 27*).

And the same great doctor also assures us that the Christian at prayer is *always* in Christ. Speaking of those who are given the grace to experience the highest forms of prayer, she says:

> You may fancy that one who has enjoyed such high favours need not meditate on the mysteries of the most sacred humanity of our Lord ... Of this at least I can assure them: they will never enter the last two mansions of the castle. If they lose their guide, our good Jesus, they cannot find the way and ... Our Lord himself tells us that he is the Way; he also says that he is the Light; that no man comes to the Father but by him; and that he who sees me, sees the Father also
> (St Teresa *Interior Castle 6,7*).

The teachings of the great Christian mystics, including our author, clearly assert the central role of Christ. Whatever similarities might exist between the phenomena of contemplative prayer among Christians and those of other great religions the Christian asserts the essential and abiding role of Christ. By clear implication this asserts the role of ordinary human experiences and things. We are led to God through such. The Christian way is a 'sacramental' way: God touches us through the visible world and we are drawn to him in and through the mystery of Christ:

> You are taught to forsake and despise your own self, according to the teaching of Christ in the gospel: 'If you will

come after me, deny yourself, take up your cross, and follow me' (Mt 16:24). In effect he is speaking of the person who will come meekly not so much with him as after him to the bliss of heaven or the mount of perfection. For Christ went ahead by nature, and we come after him by grace *(Privy Counsel 7)*.

4. In the Fullness of Time

> *(Thirdly) you should not write or speak of this matter) to anyone unless that person is, in your opinion, one who, for a long time, has been doing all that can be done to prepare for the contemplative life* (The Cloud, *Prologue*).

This particular requirement obviously speaks of someone who has some interest or discerns some call (however vague) to a deeper form of prayer. The author elaborates this in some detail in the final chapter of *The Cloud*. But he makes it very clear that this is not merely a matter of having some emotional attractions (a 'likyng steryng') when one reads about this form of prayer *(The Cloud 75)*. It is all too easy to be attracted to the idea of prayer, and to enjoy talking about it; it is another matter actually to pray. Indeed we can all too easily fall into the trap of assuming that because we have talked about a thing, we have actually done it. This is especially so regarding prayer.

The first of the more specific signs which the author gives of this call is that one is attuned to the life of the Church. But more about that later. For the present the author concentrates on one's own special grace. Anyone who feels an attraction for this form of prayer should seek to assess that urge:

> one should enquire whether this urge is pressing constantly on the attention, more so than any other spiritual exercise *(The Cloud 75)*.

Here our author shows a very great confidence in one's own spiritual experience. While he clearly does not say that such attractions are the only reliable indicator, a person can pay due heed to impulses to do what is clearly good. But he realises that this attraction might not last for very long: he does not see this loss as entirely a matter of human frailty and inconsistency. If the attraction is a grace it might well be taken away for some time. Any grace, after all, is a gratuitous gift from God. And the grace of contemplative prayer is not something that can be evoked by some elaborate technique. God has a purpose in removing the urge for a time:

> so that a person shall not become overly familiar with it, and reckon that it lies in great part in his own power to have it when and as he wishes. Such imagining is pride
> *(The Cloud 75).*

Such a withdrawal can also be caused by a person's own carelessness. In such cases the loss is felt very keenly. But that too can have a purpose.

> Sometimes our Lord delays the grace by an artful device, and by such a delay makes it grow stronger. So it becomes more deeply appreciated when it is restored
> *(The Cloud 75).*

Most of us are well aware of fluctuating attitudes to the call to prayer; sometimes we are full of enthusiasm and have a felt attraction for prayer; at other times we can successfully dodge the call by all manner of busyness. Our author is well aware of such fluctuations also. But rather than see them simply as 'our' attitudes and moods, he also prompts us to see the other side of the coin. God's grace is acting all the while; God is playing a part in these (sometimes embarrassing) emotional shifts. In some way he is using the very weaknesses we display. If through all of this there runs some thread of interest, attraction and a sense of call, then we can be confident that God is indeed calling us to deepen our prayer life, especially so when the urge to contemplation is restored. In support of this our author quotes two Church Fathers: St Gregory the Great (*Gospel Homilies II:28*) 'all holy desires grow by delay; and if they diminish by delay then they were never holy desires'. And St Augustine (*Letter of John to Parthos, IV:6*) who said 'the whole life of a good Christian is nothing else but holy desires'.

How long must one wait in this state of availability? The author answers in the *Book of Privy Counsel*:

> I say that you should do so until such time as the great rust of your carnal nature is in large part rubbed away; your director and your conscience being witness to that. And especially that you know in the depth of your heart that you are called to this by the Holy Spirit. Such a personal conviction is the safest and surest indication we can have *(Privy Counsel 10)*.

The author certainly does not mean that we should consider ourselves perfect before practising contemplative prayer: he makes it all too clear, as we shall see, that contemplation is a special means of eradicating a basic sinfulness in the human being. But this form of prayer does involve a commitment to Christ that requires a turning away from evil and a turning towards good. But our author does not make any hard-and-fast rule: what is a suitable time for one might not be so for another. Provided there is a genuine searching after wisdom through guidance, coupled with a real desire for God, then one's spiritual instincts can be trusted as an outpouring of the grace of God. Here, we have the freedom of the Spirit:

> The wind blows where it wills, and you hear the sound of it, but you do not know whence it comes or whither it goes; so it is with everyone who is born of the Spirit *(Jn 3:8)*.

The very great liberality of the author's teaching should greatly encourage us. If we have a genuine desire to follow Jesus Christ, then we can confidently follow our desires to plumb something of that Mystery. We can readily recognise whether this is a mere passing fad, a temporary attack of 'religion'; if we persevere for some time in this desire, and find delight in its return (should it have passed for a time), then we can be sure that this is a 'touch' of the Spirit; that Pentecostal wind is blowing, and we have but some slight 'sound' of it. But we know we can trust its gentle promptings.

While following our desire to deepen our prayer life, the author also tells us we must be 'doing all we can' to ensure its development. He makes it clear that before we 'contemplate' we must normally 'meditate'. That is we must pray with the mind, making an effort to clarify and deepen our basic beliefs and attitudes:

> These meditations are the most sure way a sinner has at the beginning to come to a deep spiritual knowledge of himself and God. And I really think that it would be impossible for such an understanding (though God can do just whatever he wishes) unless you have first seen and experienced by imagination and meditation the actual deeds of both yourself and God, and experienced sorrow for what was sorrowful and joy over what was joyful. Whoever does not come in through this door does not really enter the mystery at all *(Privy Counsel 9)*.

The person aspiring to a deeper prayer-life, must first spend some time in this 'learning process', coming to know the 'actual deeds' of self and God. Thus in some general sense it is necessary to 'read':

> There are occupations in which the apprentice in contemplation should be employed, namely, lesson, meditation and orison; or as they are more generally termed — reading, thinking and prayer ... beginners cannot

> think unless some hearing or reading comes first ... the clergy read books and other folk 'read' the clergy when they hear them preach the word of God *(The Cloud 35)*.

And taking up again the central focus of such learning, thinking and prayer, namely the 'actual deeds of self and God' he reminds us that Christ is the one with whom we must identify:

> They enter by the door who 'behold' the passion of Christ and sorrow over their wickedness which caused such suffering. They reprove themselves bitterly because they deserved to suffer and did not; so they experience pity and compassion for the Lord who suffered so much yet did not deserve to do so. So they lift up their hearts to contemplate the love and goodness of God ... the teaching of Christ is the door of devotion and the only real entrance in this life to contemplation *(Privy Counsel 9)*.

And here our author is in perfect harmony with the Christian tradition. St Thomas Aquinas expressed it thus:

> Because the human mind is weak, it must be led to knowledge and love of divine things through objects which are able to be perceived by the senses. Chief among these sensible objects which dispose for devotion is the passion of Christ; thus the Preface for Christmas prays 'that through knowing God visibly, we may be lifted up to the love of things invisible' *(Summa Theologiae II. II. 83.3)*.

A deep commitment to Christ, a faithful following of him as best one might, probably leads one to the grace to 'contemplate'. We are enabled to go from what is 'seen' to what is 'unseen'.

5. In the Church

> *If you would test the source of this urge (to contemplation) you should ask in the first place whether you have done all that should be done as preliminaries. That is, by cleansing your conscience according to the laws of Holy Church and seeking the advice of your spiritual director* (The Cloud 75).

Nothing could be further from the truth than to imagine that the deep personal prayer taught by the author, implies a rejection of the life of the Church. We have already seen that he began by invoking the Holy Spirit by using a liturgical prayer. He is ever at pains to ensure that the delicate balance between the personal and communal aspects of spirituality is maintained.

In this final chapter of *The Cloud*, where he rehearses some of the criteria for discerning a call to contemplation, he stresses the fact that this form of prayer takes place within the Church: this is the first criteria mentioned. The Church is the place where we come to know Christ and thus to experience reconciliation; and one's spiritual director is the point where the 'teaching church' speaks to the individual. This is pastoral care at the personal level.

He reiterates the need for seeking forgiveness in both *The Cloud* and the *Privy Counsel*. The form of prayer he teaches should not be undertaken

> until you have cleansed your conscience of all your sins according to the ordinary practice of Holy Church *(The Cloud 28).*

When we are faced with God's word, we are able to know ourselves as sinners; and we seek remedies:

> God's word, either written or spoken, is like a mirror ... and when you see in a physical or spiritual mirror, or know through someone else's teaching, just where the dirty mark is on your face ... you run off to a well and wash yourself. If this blemish is a deliberate sin, the 'well' is holy Church and the 'water' is confession. If the sin is deeply rooted, and produces evil impulses, then the 'well' is the all merciful God, and the 'water' is prayer *(The Cloud 35)*.

In all of this one notes the author's great sense of balance: there is a place for one's spiritual director: the Christian can have a personal guide and mentor who can teach the individual much; and one's own prayer also has a special role in the process of forgiveness and healing. And likewise with the Church, the whole body of Christians; to set out on the contemplative way without being alive to the grace of God in the Church would be foolhardy in the extreme:

> I take it for granted that you have already been lawfully absolved of all your sins in particular and in general, in accordance with the true teaching of Holy Church. Otherwise neither you nor anyone else would be so foolish as to undertake this work. Certainly you would not have my consent to do so *(Privy Counsel 2)*.

And in similar words the advice is repeated in the *Epistle of Prayer*. This oft repeated instruction to seek forgiveness in the Church is not merely a reflection of contemporary Church practice in the author's time. If we are to face God in prayer, then we need to be sure that our hearts have a basic godly orientation. We cannot be both for God and against God (Mt 12:30). If we come to God in prayer we cannot worship him with words only, while our hearts are

In the Church • 41

far from him (Mt 15:8). So if we have some disorientation in our attitude towards God or our fellows, then we should set things aright:

> So if you are offering your gift at the altar, and there remember that your brother has something against you, leave your gift there before the altar, and go; first be reconciled with your brother, and then come and offer your gift *(Mt 5:23-24)*.

It might be thought strange that the author, while stressing the need for confession of sins, makes little or no reference to other aspects of the life of the Church. But we need to remember that he is not writing a treatise on the Eucharist, or indeed on the Church itself. For his purpose it is sufficient to stress the basic realities regarding this life of contemplation: it takes place within Christ; and we need the grace of reconciliation which we find within the Church. To say that is to imply all that can be said about the Church.

It is in the Church that we meet Christ and are 'incorporated' into his life; it is in the Church that he reconciles us to himself, to one another and indeed to ourselves. This 'reconciliation' takes place in the first instance in Baptism where we are overshadowed by the Holy Spirit and brought to a new birth in Christ. Our lives are now intertwined with the lives of our fellow Christians:

> Just as the body is one and has many members, and all the members of the body, though many are one body, so it is with Christ. For by one Spirit we were all baptised into one body — Jews or Greeks, slaves or free
> *(1 Cor 12:12)*.

Our author is very conscious of this teaching of our fundamental unity in Christ. The one who is committed to a life of contemplative prayer is more than ever deeply aware of this personal involvement in a body, the Church:

> Just as all were lost in Adam and all who witness by their deeds to their desire for salvation, are saved by the sufferings of Christ. In somewhat the same manner, a soul that is given to this work of contemplation ... does all that it can to make all people as perfect in this work as it is itself *(The Cloud 25)*.

Thus this prayer is not a personal possession which one treasures simply for oneself. If it is genuine contemplation it displays the essential quality of 'goodness': that is, it wishes to share the blessing with others. One's concern for others in the body of Christ is deepened and sharpened through contemplative prayer:

> Just as if a limb of our body feels sore, all the other limbs are pained and diseased also, and when a limb fares well, all the others enjoy good health. It is exactly the same with the spiritual limbs of Holy Church. Christ is our head and we the limbs *(The Cloud 25)*.

The author echoes the teaching of Paul in 1 Cor 12:22 and also in Eph 5:23. This sense of belonging to the body of Christ gives an apostolic urgency to prayer; our prayer is prayer in union with Christ on the cross; it has a part to play in redeeming the world:

> If you would be a perfect disciple of the Lord you should make the effort to lift up your spirit in this spiritual exercise for the salvation of your brothers and sisters, just as our Lord lifted up his body on the cross *(The Cloud 25)*.

Indeed this prayer has some cosmic significance, influencing the whole spiritual realm. What the individual does in prayer is a matter for rejoicing throughout the entire kingdom of God, and it also has its impact on the powers of darkness and evil:

In the Church • 43

> This is a spiritual work most pleasing to God.
> All the saints and angels rejoice in this work,
> and hasten to help it in every way.
> All fiends are furious when you engage in it;
> and try to defeat it in every way they can.
> All people living on earth are
> wonderfully helped by this work,
> in ways you do not understand.
> Yes, even the souls in purgatory have
> their pain eased by the power of this work *(The Cloud 3)*.

Thus the author makes it clear that he is a devout, believing member of the Church; and membership of that body places him at the centre of the great cosmic battle between good and evil. He certainly does not conceive prayer as some form of spiritual elitism and remote individualism. He believes in being faithful to the public (presumably liturgical) life of the Church (*The Cloud 37*) and he is at great pains (doubtless in keeping with his care not to be misunderstood) to distance himself from heretics; these are guilty of 'pride and curiosity' and 'lean overly much on their own learning' *(The Cloud 56)*.

In a very moving passage the author shows how the life of prayer is really at the centre of the mystery of the Church; the Christian who prays is in deep personal contact with Christ:

> Whoever you are who feel this compelling desire to come to contemplation ... must do this: you should call together your thoughts and desires, and make them into a 'church', and therein learn to love only this good word — Jesus. You must set all your thought and desire on loving him, and do so without ceasing, as far as possible. In this way you will fulfill what is said in the psalm: 'Lord, I will praise you in the church' (Ps 26:12), that is, in thoughts and desires for the love of Jesus. And there in this 'church' of thoughts and desires and in this unity of study and will, take care that all your thought, desire,

study and will is directed solely to the love and praise of the Lord Jesus. Do all this without forgetting, as far as you are enabled by grace, and as your frailty will permit. And always humbly pray and seek counsel, patiently awaiting the will of the Lord until such time as your mind is transported out of itself, and fed with the food of angels, and you behold God and the things of God. Then will be fulfilled what is written in the psalm: 'There is Benjamin, the young child, transported out of mind' (Ps 68:27) *(Benjamin)*.

It is not often that our author alludes to the 'higher' states of prayer: this mention of being 'transported out of mind' is one of the few examples the reader will meet. And then it is merely a passing reference without any effort at close analysis or elaboration. What is far more interesting is that it is within the Church that one finds the opening to the eternal, to the growth in mystery that is involved in such 'advanced' stages of mystical prayer. It is in the Church that one meets the Lord Jesus, and it is with him, in him and through him that one enters the mystery of God. This all implies, surely, that the one committed to a Christian mysticism will keep close to Jesus Christ in word and sacrament. There is simply no other 'way'.

6. Growth in God

> *My friend in God. You shall do well to understand that according to my own somewhat crude reckoning there are four stages and degrees in the Christian life; namely Common, Special, Singular and Perfect. The former three may be begun and ended in this life while the fourth by grace may be begun here, but it shall go on forever in the bliss of heaven ... I think that according to this very same order and in the same way, our Lord, in his great mercy, called you and led you to himself by the desire of your heart* (The Cloud 1).

The author makes it clear that he does not wish this to be any more than a handy rule of thumb, a practical guide to indicate the broad outline of Christian growth. He says it is something he finds in his 'boistous beholdying' which Clifton Wolters renders as 'rough and ready way'. Even as a rough guide it certainly enables us to appreciate that growth takes place and that such growth can be discerned by a wise guide. Needless to say the author does not wish to promote any overly introspective taking of one's own spiritual temperature; hence the rather general outline of the stages of growth. He is much more concerned for the reality of God's grace: it is the Lord who, in his great mercy, calls and leads us by the desires of the heart. The wise spiritual director (such as our author obviously was) can discern that grace and growth.

A similar four-stage growth pattern is outlined by St Catherine of Siena in the *Dialogue* (chapter 56) where she distinguishes 'ordinary love' in the first place as 'those who keep the commandments in the spirit of the counsels' after which there are three other stages, 'three stairs', which she describes in suitably vague terms as imperfect (mercenary), more perfect (the faithful servant) and the most perfect (one who loves as a child without regard for self love). And she adds a wonderfully practical note: 'all three can be present in one and the same person'. So, like the author of *The Cloud*, she merely gives a rough guide, a pointer. We cannot make such outlines too rigid.

All great spiritual writers make much the same point. We who are striving to place ourselves under the influence of God's grace are growing. But at the same time we know that we are so confused and fickle that at one time we can seem godly, and shortly afterwards show a frightening and surprising destructiveness in our attitudes, words and actions. St Paul testifies to this when he says:

> I do not understand my own actions. For I do not do what I want, but I do the very thing I hate *(Rom 7:15)*.

And Julian of Norwich tells us:

> man is fickle in this life, and by his frailty and ignorance falls into sin. He is essentially weak and foolish and his will can be overborne *(Revelations 47)*.

But there is also the reality of God's grace which the author prompts us to discern. Because of God's grace we can be confident; because of our fickle nature we can never be complacent.

And so our author takes us on this journey through a four-stage growth in grace. The description of the first 'category' of persons seems understandable enough: the 'Common' are those who are Christian by commitment, but their faith is not particularly deep. It is rather like the seed scattered on the pathway and the rock (Mt 13:4-5).

Growth in God • 47

Yet such people are genuinely Christian and they perform 'good and honest bodily works of charity' *(The Cloud 8)* though in this 'lower part of the active life you are, as it were, outside yourself and beneath yourself' *(The Cloud 8)* which implies that such activity can be superficial, such a person has not really entered into self nor risen 'above' self. He reiterates this teaching in chapter 21 of *The Cloud* and further elucidates his meaning in chapters 62 and 67. Thus:

> whenever your mind is occupied with any bodily thing, however good it might be in itself, you are still 'beneath' and 'outside' yourself *(The Cloud 67)*.

The point need hardly be laboured. We can often tie ourselves in emotional knots in our concern about how we appear; what others think of us; what we have; and what we might acquire; the status we can claim; the manipulative powers we might exercise. St Teresa comments in graphic terms on this human tendency to stay on the 'edge' of our true selves:

> Rarely do we reflect upon what gifts our souls may possess, who dwells within them, or how extremely precious they are. Therefore we do little to preserve their beauty; all our care is concentrated on our bodies, which are but the coarse setting of the diamond or the outer walls of the castle ... many people live in the outer courtyard of the building where the guards stand, neither caring to enter, nor to know who dwells therein ... certain books on prayer that you have read advise the soul to enter into itself, and that is what I mean *(Interior Castle I, 1)*.

In this stage we are very concerned with 'self'; and there is a good deal of self which must grow less and less, and indeed die, if we are to come to the true freedom of the children of God. But our author takes a very realistic view and accepts us where we are, and turns it to good purpose. Indeed he is very sure that we must accept ourselves just as we are. We need to have our prayer experience

> freely anchored and grounded in true belief. Intellectually and emotionally this shall be nothing other than a naked thought and a blind acceptance of your own being *(Privy Counsel 1)*.

From this vantage point he will lead us to a deeper spirituality:

> And therefore by toil and sweat in every way you can and may, seek to obtain a true knowledge and feeling of yourself as you are. And I believe that soon after that you will have a true knowledge and feeling of God as he is *(The Cloud 14)*.

Something of the colour of the author's language, which cannot be adequately captured in modern English, can be gleaned from the original of the above question:

> Therefore swink and swete in all that thou canst and mayest, for to get thee a true knowledge and a feeling of thyself a wreche as thou art. And then I trowe that sone after that thou schalt have a trewe knowying and a felying of God as he is.

The 'swink and swete' (toil and sweat) are certainly picturesque and earthy descriptions of what the author likes to call this 'work' of contemplation. And this work of self-knowledge and self-acceptance is no easy task; we know that well enough from our experience, and that experience is reflected in the words of the author:

> I have never known a sinner come to a perfect knowledge of himself and his inner disposition, unless he had been taught it in the school of God by the experience of many temptations, fallings and risings. You know how through

the waves, floods and storms of the sea on the one hand, and the gentle wind, calm and fair weather on the other hand, the fragile ship at last reaches land and harbour. In like manner diverse temptations and tribulations, befall the soul in the ebb and flow of life. Also the goodness and grace of the Holy Spirit with his frequent visitations, sweetness and spiritual strengthening enables the fragile soul, like the frail ship, at long last to reach firm land and the haven of help. That is to say one comes to a clear and true knowledge of oneself and one's inner attitude and disposition *(Discernment of Stirrings)*.

We certainly begin with self: we are concerned about our well-being. As St Bernard tells us with disarming frankness 'We have no feeling that is not for self' (*On the Love of God, 8*). We have to be drawn through that self-interest to realise that we can only be our true selves in the wider context of God and others. We begin the journey by realising that we are people who need healing, forgiveness and true life. How else can we come to know the God who touches us as healer, the merciful one, and as the true and living God?

> I would suggest that firstly you learn to know the unseen things of your own spirit before you presume to know the unseen things of the spirit of God. For if you do not know yourself, but think you have got a fair knowledge of God, you are undoubtedly mistaken *(Benjamin)*.

This self knowledge now moves to a deeper level. The author describes the second 'stage' as Special. The person is now anxious to take the Christian life more seriously; it is no longer a matter of simply conforming to what is required, or indeed of just being content to avoid damnation. This second stage is the 'higher part of the active life' and seems to merge with the next stage, 'the lower part of the contemplative life'. Now a deeper awareness of self, others and the God of compassion emerges. There are now good spiritual thoughts, and an active appreciation of your own wretchedness, sorrow and contrition; and pity and compassion for the suffering of Christ and his servants. There is also thanks and praise for the wonderful gifts, kindness and works of God in all his creatures, both physical and spiritual *(The Cloud 8)*.

Once again there is a quite deliberate and conscious attention to Christ. And as for the self-understanding, it must be carefully noted that he does not instruct or encourage us to a morbid or long drawn-out introspective activity. He obviously speaks of a practical, down-to-earth acceptance of one's basic poverty 'nakidly as thou art', saying quite cheerfully to God 'what I am Lord I offer to you' *(Privy Counsel)*. He is very sure that once we have this basic self awareness, there is no need to probe too deeply. In very colourful language he jolts us out of any undue introspection:

> you know at least partly and I suppose as well as is profitable at this stage just what you are: a human being by nature and a foul stinking wretch by sin ... Leave well enough alone. Stir no more for fear of the stench! *(Privy Counsel 1)*.

Sensible advice. The whole message of the scriptures is that we must be aware of our need for redemption; and then turn to the Lord, not simply give way to a self analysis which can only lead to depression and despair. We must cease to do evil and learn to do good (Is 1:16-17); if the wicked man turns away from his sins, he shall live (Ezek 18:21); we must turn to the Lord our God (Hos 14:12) and the prodigal son, realising the degradation his sin entailed, came to his senses and said 'I will arise and go to my Father' (Lk 15:18). So, as we come to know ourselves and enter more deeply into the mystery of self, we realise that we are children of the Father, our lives enfolded in mercy and love: that also is part of the truth about ourselves.

Growth in God • 51

But our author wishes to probe other aspects of our being. While we are redeemed, and our duties set in this place, we carry about a special fragility: it is a good thing, he tells us, to remember that we might well die before we have completed our prayer:

> I think that what you will find very profitable at the beginning of the prayer, whether that prayer is long or short, is to be fully aware in your own heart, without any trace of self deception, that you shall die at the end of the prayer *(Epistle of Prayer)*.

He realises that this will certainly give way to some sense of dread because of one's own wretchedness. This can serve no good if it is only a foundation for more dread. It should rather prompt us to seek afresh the mercy of God. Needless to say this realisation of our tenuous grip on time can well serve to deepen our awareness of an eternal dimension which liberates us from so many of the concerns that tie us down to the edge of our true selves. We all need to give some thought to the insights which the poet so eloquently expresses: 'We have but a short span of days' (Ps 39:5); 'wise men and fools must both perish and leave their wealth to others' (Ps 49:10); 'we can be swept away like a dream, or like the grass which springs up in the morning but by evening fades and withers' (Ps 90:5-6); to sum it all up, 'we are but pilgrims on earth' (Ps 119:19). How foolish then to be like the man in the parable who strains his resources to fill ever larger barns with largely irrelevant cares and concerns, and be taken by surprise when his soul was required of him (Lk 12:20). We don't have here a 'lasting city' (Heb 13:14) however secure and comfortable we seek to make it.

Thus our author takes us on a journey of discovery or deeper awareness of ourselves; we are slowly learning to 'rise above' the many interests and attitudes which hinder our true freedom. He does not greatly distinguish the two stages Special and Solitary: they merge one into the other. Indeed he says that in these two stages

> the contemplative and active lives are coupled and knit together in a spiritual kinship and made sisters after the fashion of Martha and Mary *(The Cloud 21)*.

7. *The Best Part*

> *Whenever you find your mind occupied with nothing physical or spiritual, but only with the thought of God as he is in himself . . . then you can be said to be 'above' yourself. And indeed you are, because you can only do this by grace, not by your own powers. That is to say you are 'oned with God' in spirit, in love and in the harmony of wills* (The Cloud 67).

> *This is the 'best part' that Mary chose . . . The Lord described this as the 'best part' which shall never be taken from her. (The other parts) although they are good and holy, they terminate with this life. In the other life there will be no need (as there is now) to practise the works of mercy, to weep over our wretchedness or over the passion of Christ. For in that life there will not be any people who hunger or thirst as they do now; nor who die of the cold or be sick or homeless; nor be imprisoned as now; nor even need burial, for none shall die . . . Whoever is called to this 'best part' by God, should set about it with all vigour and joy. It shall never be taken away. It begins here and shall last for all eternity* (The Cloud 21).

Finally our author deals with the last of his four stages or categories of Christians, the 'Perfect' *(The Cloud 1)*. As is clear from the sections of *The Cloud* quoted above, the author recognises that there is a stage in our prayer when we 'transcend' ourselves; we are enabled by grace to put behind us concerns over the things that entice and preoccupy us, the worries that press upon us, the guilt feelings that can haunt us; we can even leave off anxiety and petition about the graces we feel and know we need. All manner of 'physical and spiritual' goods can be forgotten, and placed aside. We can become, as he quaintly puts it 'oned with God'; that is, just simply concerned or desiring a harmony of our will with God's will, whatever this might imply or entail.

So many of the things that concern us in our prayer are right and wholesome. Indeed our author shows that he is very much aware of the great social problems that confront the Christian. But he is consistent and adamant that at some stage of our prayer we can leave off our various involvements in such matters, 'good and holy' as they are, and experience the 'best part', the part of Mary. This is not a matter of shirking one's duties, or turning one's back upon others; this 'best part' is something to which one is called by God. And as we shall see, it does indeed come to address the great and pressing issues of the contemporary world.

Our author has schooled us to accept self and then simply to give self to God. He has also prompted us to reflect on how fragile is our grasp of time: we are transients, pilgrims. As we come to the threshold of contemplative prayer, he challenges us to heed the movement of grace and go further: to rise 'above' ourselves; to seek a radical freedom from self-centredness:

> Because you were raw and inexperienced in spiritual matters, I bade you at the beginning to enfold and clothe the awareness of God in the awareness of yourself. Yet once you have been made wiser and more pure in spirit through perseverance, you will then completely strip, spoil and divest yourself of any kind of self awareness so that you will be enabled to be clothed with the gracious

awareness of God ... seek to escape from yourself as from poison ... May Jesus help you now, for now you need him ... Now you are a cross for yourself. And this is truly the way to our Lord who said 'Let a person carry the cross' first in the very painfulness of oneself; and then 'Follow me' into joy and on to the mountain of perfection, tasting the sweetness of my love, in the experience of the divinity ... So now, utterly stripped of your self, and naked, you are clothed in God as he is in himself *(Privy Counsel 8 and 12).*

Thus our author's guidance takes us on a journey into self, through self, and then eventually to rise 'above' self. We realise that the self is the 'temple of the Holy Spirit' (1 Cor 6:19) and therefore especially graced to grow in self-awareness as an 'image' of God (Gen 1:27); the 'work of God's hand' (Is 64:8); 'crowned with glory and honour' (Ps 8:7) 'bought with a price' (1 Cor 6:20); and 'born again' (Jn 3:3). As we grow in appreciation of the gifts of God, and the gift of himself, we must also grow less self-centred. Our author clearly shows this to be the way which is Jesus Christ: we must lose our lives that we might save them (Mt 10:39). This brings us to contemplative prayer: to forget self and concentrate on God; just to *be* in the presence of God and the mystery of God.

A crucial question now presents itself. Am I called to such a prayer? Is this expecting too much? Is it not all a bit 'heady' and 'remote' from the practical living of the Christian life? We could be forgiven for thinking so. The way this matter has been treated by many writers over the last few centuries would indeed make it all sound far removed from the ordinary run of Christians. They made endless quibbles about contemplation being 'acquired' and sometimes (rarely enough) 'infused'; and the prerequisites listed generally frightened people off. There is now a healthy return to a more liberal view. Michael

Ramsey, in his typically lucid manner, sums up a more contemporary attitude:

> It would be rash of me to venture far into the controversial subject of the relation between meditation and contemplation, and between activity and passivity in prayer. But these matters are fundamental. In modern times ... there came about a tendency to regard discursive meditation (called by whatever name) as a norm for most Christians and to think of any approach to contemplative prayer as a thing far removed and characteristic of advanced souls or mystics. But we have seen the recovery of an older tradition of spirituality, whereby elementary contemplation has a place not only for advanced souls but for ordinary Christians too. This older tradition is beautifully described by Dom Cuthbert Butler, a former Abbott of the Benedictine Monastery of Downside, in his book *Western Mysticism*. I would myself humbly dare to say that whereas discursive meditation can become all too easily a cerebral process, putting too much strain upon the powers of the mind, affective prayer or elementary contemplation is God's gift to many who are ready to reach out to God in desire and longing. This contemplative prayer is something which God can grant to souls who reach out to him in their poverty, their want, their childlike desire. It is a prayer which some writers describe as coming 'from the ground of the soul'. I believe that the capacity of the ordinary Christian for contemplation is greater by far than some of our theories of the spiritual life have allowed *(Canterbury Essays and Addresses p 29)*.

During the turbulent 1960s various Church leaders issued what can well be regarded as prophetic calls to Christian people to heed the grace of contemplation. The bishops at the Second Vatican Council placed it (by implication) in the broad context of a contemporary need:

as specialisation in different branches of knowledge continues to increase so rapidly, how can the necessary synthesis of them be worked out, and how can men preserve that ability to contemplate and wonder, which leads to wisdom? *(Gaudium et Spes 56)*.

This very complexity of modern life demands quiet and reflection. And speaking in more specific terms, the Council called members of religious orders occupied in the busy round of ministries in the Church to 'combine contemplation with apostolic love' *(Perfectae Caritatis 5)*. And the Bishops of the Anglican Communion, at the 1968 Lambeth Conference called all Christians to such a form of prayer:

> The faith of the Church that God reigns and loves and speaks is sustained and renewed in its members by constant prayer. Its life is in Christ and its life is vigorous as its members try to live in and with Christ. We call all Christians to fresh efforts to deepen their prayer life, to search for those forms of prayer which are most relevant to them in their own situation, and to develop that talent for stillness in the presence of God which all possess in some degree *(The Lambert Conference 1968. Resolutions and Reports p 23)*.

And what does our author say about all this? Does he see contemplative prayer as something for the elite few? Or is it a grace given widely and generously? He seems to have a very clear view:

> In the early days of the Church in the time of persecution, many different kinds of people suddenly experienced a marvellous touch of grace. This came in a most unexpected manner and without any special preparation. Craftsmen cast aside their tools of trade and children their books and ran off without more ado to be martyred with the saints. Will you not believe that today, in times

of peace, God may, can, and indeed will and in fact does, touch different souls just as suddenly with the grace of contemplation. I certainly believe that he is willing to give this grace to his chosen souls *(Privy Counsel 6)*.

Our author encourages us by summing up the signs which indicate the presence of this grace to 'contemplate'. Towards the end of the *Privy Counsel*, he says we should subject our inclination (to use this form of prayer) to a threefold rule. It should be:

> tested by a careful examination of scripture,
> the guidance of a director, and
> your own conscience
> *(Privy Counsel 12)*.

Earlier he gave the same three pointers in *The Cloud 16*. He spoke of the guidance of a director and one's own conscience and then, not specifically mentioning 'a careful examination of scripture' he immediately launched into his detailed account of the Martha and Mary story. In his view this is obviously the special place where the scriptures teach that we can leave off our ordinary cares and concerns and be still before the Lord. Each of us has something of Martha about us: we like to fuss and bother over many things, even godly things; we are all influenced by a world in which movement and noise are often taken as symptoms of progress; and many of us like to be mobile and vocal anyway; we are certainly mostly anxious to see a job done, and done well. Yet the Gospel incident calls us to some time of utter stillness.

As to a director's guidance, perhaps most of us can be personally touched by the general guidance given by great Christian leaders: there is a need for contemplation, it is not a mere luxury. Without it we run the risk of reducing everything to the level of the trivial: without it we have not begun to wonder at the gift given us in Baptism — God himself.

And one's own conscience? What is our own experience? What are our own abilities? We need to remember that when we gaze on a beautiful mountain, without examining its details, we can be said to 'contemplate' it; we are held captive by its beauty, rather than making an inventory of its geographic, climatic or geological properties, or even thinking how it might best to put to 'use'. When we are still before God in a simple act of *being for God and with God*, then we can be said to 'contemplate'. We do not need to complicate this form of prayer: it is not beyond the capabilities of a human being graced by God.

8. Desiring God

> *Our Lord, in his great mercy, called you and led you to himself by the desire of your heart ... Through the same love by which he made you and shaped you when you were nothing, and bought you with the price of his precious blood when you were lost in Adam, he would not suffer you to be far removed from him in your lifestyle. And so in a most gracious manner he kindled your desire, and fastened you by a leash of longing, and led you by it* (The Cloud 1).

The author maintains a delicate harmony between the grace of God by which we are 'called and led', and the free will by which we respond with 'the desire of the heart'; the gift of grace is a sign of the 'great mercy' of God. And then he seeks to focus our attention on the gifts of creation and redemption, both of which show God's great love for us. There is a very tender note running through this, and one can well imagine our author viewing human creation as it is depicted in the wonderful carving on the north entrance to Chartres cathedral. There, Adam's head is held gently in the hands of the Maker who is lovingly shaping him and making him. There is no doubting that our author entertained a very lofty concept of the original human creation, prior to the Fall. Adam, he tells us in *Privy Counsel*, experienced a 'oneing affection' for God. And in very realistic terms he depicts the value of human creation:

> God fits harmoniously with our souls by adapting his Godhead to them, and our souls for their part, similarly

fit him because of the worthiness of our creation in his image and likeness *(The Cloud 4)*.

The expression that we 'fit' God and that God 'fits' us at first sounds somewhat surprising; but it is an indication of the practical bent of this author. Humanity works well when we humans are in harmony with the Creator. And the creative activity of God is a work of love. He echoes Genesis: 'he saw everything that he had made ... it was very good' (Gen 1:27,31), and also Isaiah:

> O Lord, you are our Father,
> we are the clay, you are the potter;
> we are the work of your hand
> *(Is 64:8)*.

With St Paul we recognise that we are 'his workmanship' (Eph 2:10). This image of God as craftsman, taking a loving interest in his creation is one we all need to ponder at times. Our author would certainly have us do so.

Having a positive and God-oriented view of creation gives us the foundation of our worth and self acceptance. It is the first step up the ladder to God. At the end of the first chapter of his treatise, *The Mind's Road to God*, St Bonaventure makes very clear the value he attaches to a positive view of creation:

> Whoever is not illumined by the great splendour of created things is blind,
> whoever is not awakened by such great clamour is deaf,
> whoever does not praise God because of these effects is dumb,
> whoever does not (recognise God from such great signs) is foolish
> *(The Mind's Road to God I, 15)*.

And our author sees the next god-ward step as being the gift of redemption. In *The Cloud of Unknowing 64-66* the author shows how the Fall resulted in our being 'scattered'; we lost inner unity and a clearly directed purpose; our minds were not set upon God who alone could satisfy our desires. St Augustine gives voice to this sentiment in his own deeply-felt manner:

> only in you do I find a safe haven for my mind, a gathering place for my scattered parts, where no portion of me can depart from you *(Confessions X, 40)*.

God came to us when we were 'scattered' through sin. As Bonaventure says in the work just quoted:

> when anyone lies fallen, he must remain there prostrate unless someone gives him a helping hand ... (God) assumed human form in Christ (and makes himself) a ladder, repairing the first ladder which was broken in Adam *(The Mind's Road to God IV, 2)*.

And our author echoes these sentiments:

> How right you are when you say 'for the love of Jesus'. For there, in the love of Jesus shall be your real help. There is a power in love that enables it to share everything. So love Jesus and everything that he has is yours
> *(The Cloud 4)*.

Our redemption, like our creation, shows the tender compassion God has for humanity. In our redemption he comes to us as the good shepherd seeking the one who was lost; as the good Samaritan who sees and has compassion on a broken humanity robbed of its dignity; as the Father who rejoices over the prodigal who was lost and found and who was dead and has returned to life. As our author notes in the section quoted at the beginning of this chapter, we were bought 'with the price of his most precious blood'. Here he echoes the words of St Paul:

> You are not your own;
> You were bought with a price
> *(1 Cor 6:20).*
>
> you were bought with a price,
> do not become slaves
> *(1 Cor 7:23).*

And St Peter tells us that our true freedom is that won for us by Christ:

> you were ransomed from the futile ways inherited from your fathers, not with perishable things such as silver and gold, but with the precious blood of Christ *(1 Pet 1:18-19).*

So our author teaches that the very 'same love' fashions us from nothing; redeems us from the fallen state; and continues to nurture us in a 'most gracious manner' when he kindles our desire for him and fastens us by a 'leash of longing'. Here God communes with us and makes us his friends. Thus creation, redemption, and the call to a life of prayer are three manifestations of God's providential care or stages in our growth. All three are part of our making; they show the Creator at work in the wonder of his creation, in the new birth of baptism and in the on-going 'overshadowing' by the Spirit in our life of prayer. We do well to ponder these creative gifts and so appreciate something of the Maker and indeed know him (and ourselves) the better. And we are to be willing co-operators in this creative process through this 'leash of longing'.

Many spiritual writers have seen these stages as an application of the Genesis story of creation. St Bonaventure sees this creative process culminating in the seventh stage or 'day' when we reach the peace of contemplation. And St Irenaeus places the whole process in a framework of creation when he writes:

How then shall you be made a god, when you have not yet been made a man? Or how can you be perfect who was but lately created? Or how can you be immortal if in your mortal nature you did not obey your Maker? So it must be that at the outset you should hold the rank of human being, and then afterwards partake of the divine glory. For you did not make God, rather God made you. If then you are God's workmanship, await the hand of your Maker which creates everything in due time; . . . Offer him your heart in a soft, tractable state, and preserve the form in which the Creator fashioned you, having moisture in yourself, lest by becoming hardened, you lose the impression of his fingers . . . for the moist clay which is hidden in you is hidden there by the workmanship of God *(Irenaeus, Against Heresies IV, 29)*.

By preserving the grace of our Baptism we enable the creative process to continue. And the image of God as maker and craftsman permeates and unifies the author's understanding of creation, redemption and prayer. Placing prayer in this category certainly colours our appreciation of what prayer really is. It is not so much an 'experience' we have, or indeed something we 'do'; it is more true to say that it is something that God does *to* us; it is his work; we willingly and lovingly leave him an opening to deepen and continue his creative and healing activity within us; we offer ourselves as malleable, soft clay in the potter's hands; we leave ourselves at the disposal of the creative Spirit who overshadows us. And if prayer is part of this creative process it also points to the logical conclusion that prayer has a great deal to do with the sort of people we are becoming through the influence of prayer. But in this creative work we are not entirely passive. If we are being 'led by a leash', it is a leash of 'longing'. So our author urges us:

So fast forward I pray you! Look forward and let be what is behind you; see what you lack and not what you have

> ... Your whole life now must be one of desire, if you are to reach the 'perfect' stage. This longing desire must be at work in your will, by the power of almighty God and with your own consent. One thing I must stress; he is a jealous lover and will suffer no rival, and he will not work in your will unless he is there alone with you, by himself. He asks for no help: he asks for you. He wills that you look towards him, and let him act. Your task is to guard the windows and door, against assailing flies and enemies. And if you are willing to do this, you need only meekly rest on him in prayer, and he will help you. Press ahead then, and see how you do. He is always ready and always waits for you *(The Cloud 2)*.

Our desire for God, the 'leash of longing', is something that must permeate and colour our whole selves and all that we do. And that certainly does not happen all at once. Indeed there are times when we feel several stages removed from 'wanting God'. We have to be content with 'wanting to want God'; and we might find ourselves even further back and 'wanting to want to want ...'

Sometimes we are baffled and confused by the clouds of emotion which seem to be harbingers of desires which are far removed from God. Such often seem portents of 'wants' that can all too easily crystalise into decisions that are destructive. When we calmly reflect on such turmoil we wonder how these desires could possibly be translated into the desire for God. How can we exchange these cheap counterfeits for the *real* desire, the only thing that can satisfy the human heart: the true and living God? And all too often we can be swamped by desires for 'things'; an aggressive and acquisitive society is constantly haranguing us into imagining that we 'need' this or that thing. Consequently much of our energy and longing can be sidetracked into assuaging illusory 'needs'. And once again we ask how we might escape such materialism and emerge into the true liberty enjoyed by the children of God?

As a starting point we need to be encouraged by the very fact that we ask ourselves such questions, and have such misgivings. This is an indication that God is already within us. This might just be a tiny flicker of light; a fragile sign of life. But we must remember that the life and the light are *real*, and can grow stronger and stronger yet. For the life is, in fact, that tiny seed which is the beginning of the reign of God within our hearts:

> The kingdom of heaven is like a grain of mustard seed, which a man took and sowed in his field; it is the smallest of the seeds, but when it is grown it is the greatest of the shrubs and becomes a tree ... *(Mt 13:31-2).*

And we have to face our own inner ambivalence. This tiny seed must do battle with evil. Using a different image our author says we must 'guard the windows and door, against assailing flies and enemies' *(The Cloud 2).* For there is an enemy who sows bad seed among the good (Mt 13:24-5), just as there are fish of every kind in the net (Mt 13:47). We believe that this prayer which our author teaches is a means of purifying and unifying our desiring; and the fact that we spend time in prayer is a clear indication that beneath all surface impressions and superficial attractions, there is deep within us a searching for God: 'a godly will that never consents to sin' as Julian of Norwich calls it (*Revelations 37*). Our baptismal grace is a reality; in our prayer we seek to let this basic orientation saturate our whole being. This is something that requires our active cooperation with the grace of creation and redemption: our author says we must 'work' at this matter of desiring:

> Do not give up then, but work away at it until you have this longing *(The Cloud 3).*

Our prayer is one way in which we focus our desiring on something other than pressing emotional and materialistic 'wants'; in our prayer we seek to identify with deeper longings in the human heart. And the committed Christian will also find some place for fasting and what older writers called 'almsgiving'. When we deny ourselves some food or drink we focus our desiring on God rather than on self; we do indicate that we really hunger and thirst for God. And when we are able to give something away, we focus our attention on others, and indicate our desire to be liberated from a self-centred materialism. These ascetical practices are really an integral part of the taming and schooling of our desiring.

Naturally not all our desires are evil or potentially destructive, but even the best of them can be tinged with motives that are less than godly. The most seemingly generous of deeds can be soured by a desire to manipulate people, or seek rewards for ourselves. The human heart experiences a bewildering ebb and flow or desires that need to be purified and unified. *The Cloud* expresses this feeling:

> We experience ever so many aims and desires, no more and no fewer in an hour than there are atoms in the hour. If you had been reformed by grace to the state of original innocence (enjoyed by Adam) you would always have the help of grace to be in command of such strivings of the heart. Indeed none would be passed over but all would be directed towards the sovereign of all desires and the summit of all that can be willed, namely God himself *(The Cloud 4)*.

The very complexity and variety of our desiring is itself a sign that none of these things really satisfies the longing of the human heart; none is sufficiently compelling to gain our undivided attention, and harness all the energy of our striving. Even when one or other ambition is achieved, its acquisition is hardly proportionate to the intensity of our longing or striving; the new-found goal so often and so quickly loses its attraction. We are forced to accept a basic restlessness in our hearts. The poet George Herbert identified this as a decisive point where God touches the human story; this is the experience which, if correctly interpreted, shows us that we must turn to God as the only good capable of satisfying the deepest longing of the human heart. According to Herbert, God has endowed us with all goods and blessings, but he withheld the gift of rest or contentment:

> For if I should (said he)
> Bestow this jewel also on my creature,
> He would adore my gifts instead of me,
> And rest in Nature, not the God of Nature,
>   So both should losers be.
>
> Yet let him keep the rest,
> But keep them with repining restlessnesse;
> Let him be rich and wearie, that at least,
> If goodness leade him not, yet wearinesse
>   May tosse him to my breast
>
> (George Herbert *'The Pulley'*).

We seek to form a correct view of the landscape of the human journey. On the one hand we realise our basic, human restlessness, and the extent to which we are scattered and divided. With Augustine we can say that 'My inner self was a house divided against itself' *(Confessions VIII, 8)*. But we also come to know the Lord and Lover of mankind; he knows us, the work of his hands and the sheep of his pasture. We confidently bring our scattered and divided selves to him and we understand something of our real position. We commit ourselves into his creative and healing hands. We believe that here we are being kept and saved: and there is a profound peace in such believing as Augustine testified:

> O Lord you laid your most gentle, most merciful finger on my heart and set my thoughts in order
> *(Confessions IV, 5)*.

Gradually and through time God will purify our desires and give them a unity centred on himself. He alone can do so. He alone can bring unity and peace to the strivings of the human heart. We will become more deeply convinced with the author of *The Cloud* that:

> He by himself, without the addition of anything else, and indeed no one other than he, is sufficient to satisfy, and indeed much more so to fulfil the will and desire of our souls *(The Cloud 4)*.

But 'wanting' God is also a matter of our doing something. If we wish to plumb the depths of our own being and realise that we pine for God like a 'dry weary land without water' (Ps 63:1) then we must cooperate with the grace of God and seek him on the mountain-top of prayer. We must leave aside all other 'wantings' and desires and give some time and space to seeking the mystery of God.

Part 2

Be Still and Know that I Am God *(Ps 46[45]:10)*

9. On the Mountain

> *Some think this matter of contemplation so hard and frightening that it cannot be practised without much preliminary hard work; that it is but seldom experienced; and then only in a time of ecstasy. I reply to these as well as I can: Whether this grace of contemplation and the working of the Holy Spirit is given to people depends entirely on the will and good pleasure of God and also on their own spiritual state.*
>
> *There are some who cannot reach this state without long spiritual preparation, and even then they have it but seldom and as a special call from the Lord. The full perfection of this work we call ecstasy.*
>
> *There are others so graced in spirit and so at home with God in this gift of contemplation, that they may have it when they will and in the ordinary round of human conditions: whether walking, standing or kneeling. Yet in such times they have full control over their physical and spiritual wits, and many use them as they wish, though not without some difficulty, yet without great difficulty.*
>
> *We have an example of the former kind in Moses and the latter kind in Aaron, the priest of the temple* (The Cloud 71).

While preserving the primacy of God's grace, our author makes it abundantly clear that there is no one single pattern in this matter: humans differ. On the one hand he is willing to allow that due to a mysterious combination of grace, temperament and opportunity some people can experience this form of prayer readily enough; but on the other hand some need long preparation. Aaron is an example of the former but he has an obvious fondness for Moses. Moses had to undergo long preparation involving much effort before he could practise contemplation, and as such he is closer to most of us. We can readily identify with Moses; the Aarons of this world seem somewhat remote.

He then tells us that ecstasy is the full perfection of this work of prayer, but he says very little about this. As we have seen he describes Benjamin as being 'transported out of mind' (*Benjamin*) but one has the clear impression that he is not interested in such matters nor indeed in any extraordinary manifestations of religious experience. His whole emphasis is on the 'ordinary'; to stress the primacy of love; the sort of prayer which is the 'best part' chosen by Mary, and which 'begins here and shall last for all eternity' (*The Cloud 20*). This is a sufficiently general description to encompass elementary contemplation which all or most of us can practice, and those higher reaches of prayer scaled only by the chosen few.

Aaron is obviously one of those especially chosen humans whose whole life seems to be in harmony with God: there is an habitual awareness of the mystery in which they walk, though they still have their 'wits' about them. They have some difficulty, though not *great* difficulty, in keeping this extraordinary poise between everyday events and the abiding closeness of God. But they are not the norm, nor held out to us as the ideal. In treating of these biblical figures who are 'types' of this form of prayer, the author also mentions Bezaleel (Ex 31:2; 36:1 and 38:22). He has both the 'Spirit of God' and also 'ability and intelligence' and so he is one who has this contemplative ability through a clear blend of grace and diligence and who can learn much from others well practised in this form of prayer.

> Sometimes we grow in this grace through our own spiritual skill helped by grace. Then we are like Bezaleel, who did not see the Ark until he had made it by means of his own effort, though he was guided by the pattern shown to Moses on the mountain *(The Cloud 73)*.

While he does not dwell on Bezaleel as a useful guide for us, he does find a lesson in the image of the Ark:

> This grace of contemplation is symbolised by the Ark of the Covenant in the Old Law; and those who work at contemplation are prefigured by those who were responsible for the Ark ... It is fitting that this grace and work of contemplation is likened to the Ark. For just as the Ark contained all the jewels and relics of the temple, so also this little love contains all the virtues of a man's soul, and the soul is the spiritual temple of God *(The Cloud 71)*.

The image of the ark is conflated with that of the human being as the temple of the Holy Spirit (1 Cor 3:16). Our author has brought us back to the realisation that we seek the presence of God within our own selves. The journey up the mountain is just another way of describing the journey to the depths of one's being where the Lord resides.

> Before Moses could see this ark and learn how to make it, he had to make the prolonged effort to reach the top of the mountain and dwell there and work in a cloud for six days, and wait, until on the seventh day the Lord kindly showed him the manner of this ark-making. This long work and delayed vision of Moses symbolises those who cannot reach this spiritual work of contemplation without much preliminary effort, and even then they experience it but rarely, and when God wills to give it *(The Cloud 71)*.

Moses learnt this mysterious 'ark-making' on the holy mountain. The mountain symbolises both the effort that is required to reach the summit, and also the fact that such a lofty place is not our ordinary habitat, it is beyond the reach of our natural abilities. But it is only there, on the mountain top, that we learn the truth about ourselves, for the individual is the ark, the place where God resides.

In his translation and adaptation of the work by Dionysius, the author gives us a more complete picture of Moses at prayer. Moses, 'the mildest of men' was commanded by God to cleanse himself, keep clear of all defilement, and then

> he heard trumpets of many voices, and saw many shining lights, which sent out wide beams and after that he had to separate himself from his people *(Denis Hid Divinity 1)*.

Clearly Moses realised that he was called by God: by some sight and sound he was bidden to 'separate' himself. The dramatic language only highlights the fact that we do receive a 'movement of grace'. Something quite 'ordinary' that we hear might well strike us with the vigour of a trumpet's blast: God breaks in upon us by means of a casual word, a challenging word, maybe even a word that hurts.

Or something commonplace strikes us with a new intensity: God breaks through into our ordinary experience by means of some new awareness that has all the clarity of a bright light. And God asks us to 'separate' ourselves; to leave off the ordinary tasks, the everyday concerns, the things that captivate us sometimes to the point of ensnaring us. As God breaks in upon us we turn to him, speak to him, respond verbally to his presence, seek to understand the message he gives us, and search for practical steps to take. But sometimes we are unable to 'say' anything else, think more deeply, or discern practical decisions to make. We simply exhaust our human resources, we are confronted with something unseen; we face a challenge that defies a neat solution; we are baffled by something larger than ourselves which we cannot manipulate or dodge. At such a time we can follow the path of Moses:

> he attained the heights of the divine ascent which is the limit and boundary of human understanding; and this he did with the help of grace ... He was contemplating an object, not God himself, for he may not be seen by the human eye, but Moses saw the place where God is ... It was at this time that Moses with his singular affection was separated from the chosen priests and entered by himself the darkness of unknowing, a darkness which indeed is hidden, and in which one shuts out all knowable knowing ... and as he cast aside all knowing that is knowable he was united (knittyd) to God in the best possible manner, and because he knew nothing he was enabled to know what is beyond understanding *(Denis Hid Divinity 1).*

The time had come for Moses to cast aside all 'knowing'; and the use of all words that he could comprehend and control; and the framing of decisions that he could master; and the weaving of all 'pictures' he could imagine. He now had to confront the mystery of God; and in some sense pass 'beyond understanding' and be immersed in the all pervading and enveloping mystery. It is eminently understandable that Christian writers have looked to Moses as *the* example of the one who casts aside all pressing human concerns and ascends the mountain of prayer whose summit is swathed in those mysterious clouds which give us some 'image' of the mystery of God. St Gregory of Nyssa (d 395) developed this thought in his treatise *The Life of Moses*:

> What does it mean that Moses entered the darkness and then saw God in it? What is now recounted seems somehow to be contradictory to the first theophany, for then the Divine was beheld in light but now he is seen in darkness ...

> For leaving behind everything that is observed, not only what sense comprehends but also what the intelligence thinks it sees, it keeps on penetrating deeper until by the intelligence's yearning for understanding it gains access to the invisible and the incomprehensible, and there it sees God. This is the true knowledge of what is sought; this is the seeing that consists in not seeing, because that which is sought transcends all knowledge, being separated on all sides by incomprehensibility as by a kind of darkness. Wherefore John the sublime, who penetrated into the luminous darkness, says, *No one has ever seen God*, thus asserting that knowledge of the divine essence is unattainable ... When, therefore, Moses grew in knowledge, he declared that he had seen God in the darkness, that is, that he had then come to know that what is divine is beyond all knowledge and comprehension, for the text says, *Moses approached the dark cloud where God was*. What God? He who *made darkness his hiding place*, as David says, who also was initiated into the mysteries in the same inner sanctuary
>
> (Gregory of Nyssa, *Life of Moses II, 162-164*).

The image of Moses on the mountain prompts the Christian to think of that other mountain where he also figured: the mount of Transfiguration. There, the chosen friends of Christ, Peter, James and John, also 'separated' themselves from the din and clamour of their busy world and ascended the mountain. They then realised something of the meaning and the beauty of the Lord, and Peter was prompted to say 'Lord it is good for us to be here': good to be in the company of Jesus and recognise that he is the 'light of the world' (Jn 8:12); good to know that in him there is the fulfilment of the law given to Moses and the message entrusted to the prophets such as Elijah; good to see a new beauty in the simple things of life for the Lord's garments became 'intensely white, as no fuller on earth could bleach them' (Mk 9:3); it is good to be enlightened. But that was not the sum of the Christian experience on the mount of Transfiguration. As Luke recounts it:

> a cloud came and overshadowed them; and they were afraid as they entered the cloud *(Lk 9:34)*.

There, in the company of Jesus, they entered the cloud, just as Mary went 'further' than Martha and entered the mystery of Jesus. Here, too, we are invited to move beyond sight, understanding, feeling and all that can be reduced to a merely 'practical' approach. To the disciples on the mount of transfiguration it was a frightening experience. It *can* be a frightening experience to lose one's grip on the familiar; we all like to have our reassuring points of reference. Yet this experience of darkness, whether occasioned by the circumstances of life or more directly by the movement of grace in one's prayer, is the place where God dwells. The darkness is not dark to God, and the night is as clear as the day (Ps 139:12); the cloud that envelopes might seem frightening at first, but it shrouds the one whose face we cannot see and still live. It can eventually become the thing that enables us to 'see' God in what Gregory of Nyssa calls 'the seeing that consists in not seeing' and the 'luminous darkness'.

For Peter, it resulted in some deepening of faith, and indeed as a 'light':

> we were with him on the holy mountain. And we have the prophetic word made more sure. You will do well to pay attention to this as to a lamp shining in a dark place, until the day dawns and the morning star rises in your hearts *(2 Pet 1:18-19)*.

10. The Cloud

Lift up your heart to God with a meek stirring of love and mean God himself and none of his goods ... Work away at it until you have this longing. When you first do this you will find only a darkness, a cloud of unknowing as it were. You do not know what this is, saving that you feel in your will a naked intention reaching out to God. Whatever you do this darkness and this cloud is between you and your God and prevents you from seeing him in the clear light of understanding or feeling him in the sweet love of your affections. So brace yourself to remain in this darkness as long as you can, all the while crying to him whom you love. If ever you are to feel him or see him in this life, it must always be in this cloud and in this darkness (The Cloud 3).

This is our author's first explicit mention of contemplative prayer, and as an introduction it has a decidedly 'liturgical' ring to it. In the Mass, at the beginning of the Preface, we are invited to 'Lift up your hearts': as we enter the hub of this great mysterious action our sights and thoughts must be set firmly on what is unseen. We press forward, beyond the familiar and the known, even though we start with them.

In contemplative prayer, we likewise set our hearts upon what is unseen. We are not concerned to ask God for this or that blessing: we move beyond that and simply want God himself. Clifton Wolters translates this opening sentence as:

> Lift up your heart to God with humble love: and mean God himself and not what you get out of him.

In this prayer we simply want God. We do not wish to use words *about* God, for no words can adequately describe God. Here, there is need for a deep human silence. St Gregory of Nyssa tells us that we cannot know God, he is beyond our powers of knowing, and beyond the ability of human descriptive powers.

> When there is a question of God's 'godliness', then is the time to keep silence. When, however, it is a question of his operation, a knowledge of which can come down even to us, that is the time to speak of his omnipotence by telling of his works and explaining his deeds, and to use words to that extent
> (Gregory of Nyssa, *Commentary on Ecclesiastes, 7*).

Here, in contemplative prayer, we are not concerned with the many great things God has done for us: his 'operations ... works ... (and) deeds' as Gregory of Nyssa calls them. We do not concentrate on the many manifestations of God's beauty, love and goodness; here we are mute and still before the one who gives us all these good things. We are concerned not with the gifts but with the giver of all good gifts. We stand before the unfathomable presence we praise in the hymn:

> Immortal, invisible, God only wise
> In light inaccessible hid from our eyes,
> Most blessed, most glorious, the Ancient of Days,
> Almighty, victorious, thy great name we praise.

Here our human language falters and proves inadequate. Any words seem to make a triviality of the experience, even more than our feeble and trite comments could belittle a great work of art or a majestic view. We simply cannot say what is adequate. This is not an unusual human experience. And it is especially so when we confront the reality of God, no words can do full justice to the mystery. When we stand before God, our author says we must have a 'naked intention'. We do not attempt to clothe our attitude with images or words, they are too shoddy by far; nor do we seek to swathe ourselves in comforting emotions, they soon prove threadbare; nor do we equip ourselves with 'meaningful' theological insights, these will only serve to muffle the mystery. The author's carefully chosen phrase 'naked intention' is eminently practical. We simply strip ourselves of our 'clear light of understanding' and the 'sweet love of (our) affections'. And being intellectually and emotionally 'naked' we make a conscious and determined desire to 'want' God. We brace ourselves to stay in this position as long as necessary, and we concentrate our whole being on crying to him; loving him; standing silent and motionless before the mystery, the 'cloud of unknowing'.

So our author makes it very clear that in this prayer we simply focus our attention on the mystery of God. Our senses (sight, hearing, taste, feeling and smell) can only serve to give us an introduction to, or a series of hints about, God. When we see a signpost saying 'Moscow 2,000 km' we 'know' this is the road to Moscow; following it will bring us there. But the sign is not the place itself, we have not yet arrived as we read the signpost. When we use words and images they point the way to God. But they are not God.

We know, of course, that we must use words about God and employ images of God. Julian of Norwich, for example, speaks of God being

> Maker ... Keeper ... Lover ... Father ... Mother ... Husband ... Brother ... and our Saviour too
> *(Revelations 5 and 52).*

Few writers have employed such colourful and heart-warming images of God as Julian did, yet she also realised that our words and images can only take us so far and no further:

> Man in this life is blind and cannot see God, our Father, as he is ... and whenever he wills of his goodness to show himself to man, he shows himself in great simplicity, as man *(Revelations 52)*.

In contemplative prayer, then, we have travelled as far as we might along the pathway of signs, words and images. Now we stand on the threshold of mystery, unable to comprehend; yet at the same time very sure of the presence of the unseen God. Our author expresses it thus:

> Senses give no real knowledge of God ... and therefore St Denis said 'the most godlike knowledge of God is that which is known by unknowing' *(The Cloud 70)*.

If then we cannot form basic ideas of God from what the senses supply, how can we think about God? Our author poses the problem and answers it thus:

> But now you ask me and say: 'How am I to think of God himself and what he is?' and to this I cannot but answer: 'I do not know' *(The Cloud 6)*.

In her translation of *The Cloud* Evelyn Underhill retains the original word for know, 'wote' and translates this as 'I wot not'.

This terse statement helps us focus attention on what has always been affirmed by Christian theology: God is unknowable and incomprehensible, even though we can have (and indeed at times must employ) images of what God is 'like'.

St Thomas Aquinas reminds us how limited are our powers of knowing when he asserts that the revelation we have concerning God is a 'kind of clouded awareness mixed up with darkness' (*Concerning Truth XII, 12*). And St John of the Cross affirms the same truth when he says:

> (No) ideas can serve the intellect as a proximate means leading to God. In order to draw nearer to the divine ray the intellect must advance by unknowing rather than by desire to know, and by blinding itself and remaining in darkness ... *(Ascent of Mount Carmel, II, 9, 5).*

And commenting on such prayer one modern author, Abbot John Chapman, has expressed it thus:

> The strangest part is when we begin to wonder whether we mean anything at all, and if we are addressing anybody, or merely using a formula without sense. The word 'God' seems to mean nothing. If we feel this we are starting on the right road, and we must beware trying to think what God is, and what he has done for us ... *(Spiritual Letters p 120).*

And an ancient Christian writer has remarked 'Whoever sees nothing in prayer, sees God'.

However we express it, these writers are all attempting to assert that God is a mystery beyond our understanding. The important question is not how much we understand, or how clever are our words about God. The important thing is that we love him. And that is precisely what writers like the author of *The Cloud* seek to emphasise. As we face this 'darkness' and the mystery we do not seek to understand, or make fine speeches, we seek to love:

> Endeavour to pierce that darkness above you. Strike that thick cloud of unknowing with the sharp dart of longing love. And do not leave this for anything that may happen *(The Cloud 6).*

This 'sharp dart of longing love' is the way we turn our whole selves towards God. We simply love him. This indeed is the very first of the Lord's commandments — to love the Lord our God ... And so our author succinctly says:

> He can certainly be loved, but not thought,
> He can be taken and held by love but not by thought
> *(The Cloud 6).*

Indeed this love for God is the one thing that can fulfil the deepest human longings:

> Regarding our powers of knowing, God, who made our faculties, remains ever incomprehensible; and to the other power, that of loving, to each and every person he is completely knowable. One loving soul, alone, because of love, can fully comprehend him who is entirely sufficient (and much more so) without limit — to fill all the souls of men and angels that could ever exist. This is the endless and marvellous miracle of love, which shall never have an end ... the experience of this is endless happiness and the privation of it is endless suffering *(The Cloud 4).*

Thus the author reiterates his view that we cannot know God, but we can love him. The emphasis is always on the will — our loving response to God; we are not called to great knowledge of God in any learned manner, but we are called to love God with our whole heart. As we grow in this love we thereby gain some 'knowledge' of God. We can appreciate God; we have a deepening confidence in his love for us; we know that he is the one who strengthens us to avoid evil and enables us to do good. All this is 'knowledge' of a practical kind. It was this deep conviction of faith that enabled Abraham to follow God's call; it is the same conviction we find in all great Christian mystics. Time and again St Teresa of Avila, for instance, speaks of her 'confidence' in God. And Julian of Norwich spoke of our need to 'go forward intelligently and firmly' along this path of faith.

All too often we want to reduce God to 'manageable' proportions; to have some tangible and clear ideas that will satisfy. But our author warns against any efforts to be too literal in our pictures of what God is like:

> Do not think that because I call this a darkness or a cloud, that it is like a cloud formed by vapours in the air; nor like the darkness such as you have in your house at night when the light is extinguished. For such a darkness and such a cloud can certainly be imagined in your mind's eye on the brightest of summer days; and likewise on the darkest of winter nights you can imagine a clear shining light. Do not be concerned about such falsehood. I am not speaking about that at all. For when I say darkness I mean a lack of knowing; everything that you do not know or that you have forgotten is 'dark' to you because you do not see it with your spiritual eye. For this reason it is not called a 'cloud' in the sky but a cloud of unknowing that is between you and your God *(The Cloud 4)*.

The simple example he provides is significant. This 'unknowing' is like what we do not know or have forgotten. We can easily recognise ourselves as people with a capacity for forgetting! And we also have a 'capacity' for not knowing. All this tells us something about ourselves as limited and fragile. But the acceptance of our limitations is the precise point where we can meet God; this is where we must leave off any reliance on our own imagined resources and meet the unknowable, the mystery. Here we are at the frontiers where our experience borders the land of mystery. At once we are realistic enough to accept our limitations and also bring them into living touch with the one who is creating, redeeming and communing with us. So our author advises:

> See that nothing remains in your working mind but a naked intention reaching out to God, not clothed in any special thought of God, what he is or how he works, but only *that* he is ... This naked intention, freely fastened and grounded in true belief, shall be nothing other in your thought and feeling than a naked thought and a blind feeling of your own being. It is just as if you said to God 'What I am Lord, I offer to you, without thinking

of any particular quality of your being, but only that you are'. Let that meek darkness be your mirror and completely fill your mind. Think no more of yourself than you do about God so that you are one with him in spirit, without any separation or scattering of your mind. For he is your being and you are what you are in him ... so your thoughts will not be scattered and divided but centred on him who is all; always remembering this difference between you and him, that he is your being and not you his *(Privy Counsel 1)*.

While reiterating the primacy of his act of love, the 'naked intention reaching out to God', our author adds a new note here, and emphasises a basic realism. We must take the facts as they are: we accept our own existence, and we accept the existence of God. We take ourselves as we are, and we offer ourselves to God. In this act we are gathering our 'scattered' and 'separated' selves and centering ourselves on God. So we accept this limited self which can know and achieve so little and we turn our whole being towards God. Our author will certainly bid us forget self (*The Cloud 43*), but at the beginning we quite deliberately accept self and offer self to God. This of course, is the primary act of love.

As people who only see as in a mirror, dimly (1 Cor 13:12) we stand before the mystery of God. We confront the darkness or the unknowing, and we direct our loving attention to this mysterious presence which we cannot comprehend. This is a prayer which we can call a prayer of 'simple regard' or 'loving attention' or by the rather more pretentious name, 'acquired contemplation'. In our Western Catholic tradition we have one form of prayer where this is a fact and a lived experience for many of us; the tradition of prayer before the Blessed Sacrament. Here we begin (as our prayer always must) with what is near and tangible: we hear the word of God; we take bread and wine, the fruit of the earth and the work of human hands;

we bless them in obedience to the Lord's command and in the calling down of the Holy Spirit they are, as St Ambrose said, 'transfigured' into the body and blood of Christ whose death we proclaim until he comes again.

In all this we accompany Christ (as our prayer always does) and with him we approach the darkness and the mystery of God. When we pray before the blessed Sacrament we are indeed confronting a 'cloud of unknowing'; this has traditionally been called *Mysterium Fidei*, 'the mystery of faith'. Many people find it both possible and useful simply to 'be' in the presence of the Sacrament; often this is just a general and unformulated desire to love God; it is most certainly the prayer taught by the author of *The Cloud*. In the stillness and the darkness of this sacramental 'cloud of unknowing' we make our own the sentiments of St Thomas Aquinas:

> Godhead here in hiding, whom I do adore
> masked by these bare shadows, shape and nothing more,
> see, Lord, at thy service low lies here a heart
> lost, all lost in wonder at the God thou art.

11. Loving Presence

> *This is the most worthwhile searching and seeking for God that can be achieved or learnt in this life ... Yes, even though a soul which so seeks, sees nothing that may be understood by the spiritual eye of its reason. For if God is your love and your purpose, the chief aim or object of your heart, it is sufficient for you in this life ... Such a blind shot with the sharp dart of longing love will never miss its mark, which is God himself. He himself has assured us of this in the* Canticle of Canticles *(4:9) when he speaks of the languishing loving soul: 'You have wounded my heart my sister, my friend, my spouse, you have wounded my heart with but one of your eyes.' There are two eyes of the soul: reason and love. By reason we can trace how mighty, how wise, and how good he is in his creatures, but not in himself. But when reason fails, then love is anxious to live and learn to act. For by love we may find him, feel him, and touch him just as he is*
> (Discernment of Stirrings).

In this section the author quotes from the 'Song of Songs' the Old Testament book which speaks so eloquently and passionately of human love, and in so doing points to human love being a reflection of the love between God and his people and between God and the individual human being. The author freely adapts the text to suit his purposes; but the fact that he uses this at all indicates the true setting in which he wishes us to understand the love of which he speaks. When we place ourselves in the presence of the 'unknown', or the 'cloud of unknowing' we are engaging in a love affair with God. We direct towards God this 'blind shot', our love, which he describes as a 'sharp dart of longing love'. And he assures us that as we direct our love towards this darkness and this mystery it 'will never miss its mark, which is God himself'.

St John of the Cross uses similar language to describe what he also sees as a love affair with God.

In his poem *The Ascent of Mount Carmel*, he speaks of a 'night' in which the Christian meets the Beloved. Here, as is usual in such mystical language, the human being is referred to as feminine:

> In that happy night,
> In secret, seen by none,
> Seeing nought myself,
> Without other light or guide
> Save that which in my heart was burning.
>
> That light guided me
> More surely than the noonday sun
> To the place where He was waiting for me,
> Whom I knew well,
> and where none appeared.
>
> O, guiding night
> O, night more lovely than the dawn;
> O, night that hast united
> The Lover with His beloved,
> And changed her into her love.

For John of the Cross, too, the Song of Songs provides a literary background against which he writes, and a mode of expression to carry his thoughts.

The heart which is directed towards God has such a 'burning' desire for God that the very desire becomes a light in the darkness for 'that light guided (the human soul) more surely than the noonday sun'. Not only is it a guiding principle but it is also a thing of great beauty: 'more lovely than the dawn'. Yet it still remains dark, a mystery beyond our comprehension, shrouded in a cloud.

The image of a 'cloud' is indeed an apt one to describe the 'hidden God' (Is 45:15). Moses climbed the mountain of prayer 'and the cloud covered the mountain' (Ex 24:15); this cloud was covering the presence of God who 'descended in the cloud' (Ex 34:5). The cloud obviously denoted a 'holy place' (Lev 16:2); when it filled the house the 'priests could not stand to minister because of the cloud, for the glory of the Lord filled the house of the Lord' (1 Kings 8:10). Entering the cloud meant a deep personal encounter with God for 'God came down in the cloud and spoke to (Moses)' (Num 11:25) and indeed we know that the Lord spoke to Moses 'as a man speaks to his friend' (Ex 33:11).

Following this 'cloud of unknowing' and indeed entering it, is to walk by faith. And there is a special blessedness attached to this: 'Blessed are those who have not seen yet believe' the Lord said to Thomas (Jn 20:29) and Peter has a similar word for those who walk the way of Jesus Christ in the darkness of faith:

> Without having seen him you love him; though you do not now see him you believe in him and rejoice with unutterable and exalted joy. As the outcome of your faith you obtain the salvation of your souls *(1 Pt 1:8-9)*.

In this darkness of faith, the soul of the believing Christian is being 'changed into her love' as St John of the Cross expresses it; this is the 'salvation of our souls' to which Peter refers; and our author tells us that this form of prayer is something which 'begins here and shall last for all eternity' (*The Cloud 20*).

So this darkness is not a frightening absence or a void. It is eternal life in embryo; it is the very 'substance' of the 'things hoped for' (Heb 11:1). We do not seek to understand this mystery in which we are enveloped. Rather we strive to give ourselves in love to the mystery. And as we remain quiet, still and patient before this enveloping darkness we begin to have some small hints or a deepening conviction of the beauty and love with which we are surrounded. What might seem at first to be a 'nothing' attracts us with greater appeal:

> Do not worry if you cannot understand this 'nothing'; it is for this reason that I love it so much the better. It is so worthwhile a thing in itself, that (you) can have no understanding of it. This 'nothing' can be better felt than seen: for it is completely unseen and dark to those who have been looking at it for only a short while. Yet, to speak more accurately, it is an overpowering spiritual light that blinds the soul that is experiencing it, rather than actual darkness or lack of physical light. Who then is calling it 'nothing'? Surely it is our 'outer' self and not our inner self. Our inner self calls it 'All' for because of it you are learning to know the secret of all things, both physical and spiritual, without any special knowledge of any one thing in itself *(The Cloud 68).*

The basic image that he uses here is one well attuned to our ordinary experience. If we are in a darkened room for some time and then suddenly face the light, we are blinded. The light is too much for us; our faculties are seeking to be attuned too quickly to the changed circumstances; they break down under the impact. This has provided Christian writers with a suitable image for our knowledge and appreciation of God. We simply cannot cope with the 'brightness'; it is too much for our limited faculties.

T.S. Eliot once said that 'Humankind cannot bear very much reality. We have to be trained to encounter it'. But when we encounter the darkness we are not merely confronting some inability of our own. That is only one facet of it. It is also the 'darkness where God is' a darkness which is 'unknown and unseen' according to St Gregory of Nyssa (*Life of Moses II, 152, 169*). St Makarios of Egypt (c. 300-390) made this the basis of his understanding of St Paul's experience:

> the light that illumined St Paul on the road to Damascus (Acts 9:3) the light through which he was raised to the third heaven where he heard unutterable mysteries (2 Cor 12:4), was not merely the enlightenment of conceptual images or of spiritual knowledge. It was the effulgence of the power of the Holy Spirit shining in His own person in the soul. Such was its brilliance that corporeal eyes were not able to bear it and were blinded (Acts 9:8); and through it all spiritual knowledge is revealed and God is truly known by the worthy and loving soul
> *(The Philokalia III, 348).*

And St John of the Cross adopts a similar homely image:

> just as the sun is total darkness to the eyes of a bat, so the brightest light in God is complete darkness to our understanding . . . the loftier and clearer the things of God are in themselves, the more unknown and obscure they are to us . . . The Apostle also affirms this teaching: That which is highest in God is least known by men (Rom 11:33) *(The Ascent of Mount Carmel II, 8).*

And our author seeks to show by a simple illustration this blinding light is nothing other than this creative, healing and loving work of God which at times must seem to us a very painful experience indeed. In treating this he changes his image to that of a frightening storm. We are being stripped of what he has already called our 'outer' self so that our 'inner' self can come to true life. Here he echoed the words of St Paul (2 Cor 14:16). Being weaned away from what is transitory and schooled in the things of God involves a journey away from what is familiar and customary into the mystery of God. The journey is sometimes a painful one:

> Now you are on the spiritual sea, sailing from the physical to the spiritual. Many great storms and temptations will arise at this time perhaps, and you will not know where to run for help. Everything has gone: common and special grace are not in your feeling. Don't be overly fearful, even if you think you have every reason to be so. But rather have a loving trust in our Lord however little you may feel, for he is not far away from you. He will look up, perhaps very soon, and again touch you with that same grace in a more fervent way than ever you had before. Then you will think that you are whole and good enough while it lasts. For suddenly, almost before you are aware, all is swept away and you are left destitute in your boat, blown about in blind motion, hither and thither, you don't know where or whither. Don't be abashed! He will come, I promise you, very soon. Indeed. whenever he likes and will powerfully rescue you from all your grief more effectively than he ever did before *(Privy Counsel 12)*.

So our author is very clear that this time of darkness can be a time of great pain. But the pain is an essential part of the creative, healing process, and it takes place within the context of God's unbounded love for us. The illustration he uses in the above passage evoke some clear images: one can obviously see possible allusions to the Lord, asleep in the storm-tossed boat (Mt 8:23-27). That incident suggests the dark clouds of a storm; the uncertainty occasioned by the threatening waves and ferocious winds; the inability to discern clearly the active presence of the Lord; the disciples emotional reaction that prevented their seeing this as part of God's 'saving' plan — indeed it seemed the very antithesis of salvation. And so the 'intervening high and wonderful cloud' as our author calls it (*The Cloud 17*), can sometimes be so bright that we cannot glean any hint of the glory of God. Indeed there are times when it appears as a painful experience: sometimes our emotional state clouds the truth, but always the love of God is at work. As we seek to appreciate this cloud as a painful experience, we need to recall the accounts of the crucifixion given by the three synoptics:

> there was a darkness over the land until the ninth hour (Mt 27:45); there was a darkness over the whole land until the ninth hour (Mk 15:33 and Lk 23:44).

And the Lord also experienced the cloud and the darkness as is clear in his cry 'My God, my God, why have you forsaken me?' (Mt 26:46 and Mk 15:34). And Luke gives us the Lord's practical solution to the pain and the darkness: 'Father, into your hands I commit my spirit' (Lk 23:46).

We must not romanticise away the harsh realities of the crucifixion. This was a time of darkness when so many of the Lord's disciples fled in fear; to many people this death seemed sheer 'folly' and a 'stumbling-block' (1 Cor 1:20-23); it was seen as the final defeat of Christ who could help others but could not save himself (Lk 23:35). But to those prepared to walk by faith this time of darkness is also the mainfestation of the power of God to save (1 Cor 1:24); this darkness of defeat when one 'emptied himself ... and became obedient unto death' (Phil 2:7-8) is also the revelation of the love of God at work in the world. Thus our moments of darkness and pain can also screen the most dramatic moments of love.

In those dark moments which seem like our own personal crucifixion, we need to have a humble submission to the will of God and place ourselves in his hands. Our author is very sure that this has its effect:

> This humility deserves to have God himself come in his might to avenge you of your enemies, to take you up and

cherish you and to dry your spiritual eyes just as a father does for a child that is at the point of perishing in the jaws of wild boars or mad, biting bears *(The Cloud 32)*.

So when we stand before the 'cloud of unknowing' we are, as it were, in the presence of one who is playing a game of hide-and-seek with us. It is one whose attitude towards us is best summed up, if we must use human language, as a loving parent dealing with a child. This is especially so when the darkness and the pain seem to be at their most intense and most threatening. We must not be surprised at such images:

> You might think this is somewhat childishly and foolishly spoken. Yet I believe that whoever had the grace to do and feel as I say, would find that this game was well worth playing with him, just as a father plays with a child, kissing and embracing him *(The Cloud 46)*.

So in practice our attitude must be one of being still before God; not necessarily thinking fine thoughts or using many words; but just silently loving him, fixing our desiring on him, just simply wanting him. Our author has a favourite saint as a model for this attitude, in the Mary and Martha story:

> Do as Mary did. Set the aim of your heart upon one thing for 'one thing only is necessary' (Lk 10:42): namely God. It is him you want, him you seek, him you long to love, him you long to feel, him you long to embrace *(Discernment of Stirrings)*.

In contemplative prayer we follow the example of Mary. We are at the feet of Jesus and it is through our life in him that we come face to face with the mystery of God. So such prayer is nothing more than a deep stillness and silence before God. We reach out to that 'darkness' or that mystery with the one thing at our disposal — our love.

We want the one thing necessary — God. We enter the depths of our heart and seek to be in touch with the deepest facet of our being — the very core and centre of our selves, that place where the Holy Spirit has placed the ability to love (Rom 5:5).

St Matthew records Christ's teaching on the need for a religion that is not merely a matter of external observances but must strike to the very depths of our being. In this context he has much to say about our prayer. Just as when giving alms, we should not trumpet the fact abroad, so also when praying we should not seek to give good impressions to others. Rather, he says:

> when you pray, go into your room and shut the door and pray to your Father who is in secret; and your Father who sees in secret will reward you *(Mt 6:6)*.

In heeding the call to contemplative prayer, we enter this darkness, the 'room' where God dwells. If at times it is a painful experience, it is always an experience of the Father's loving care for us.

12. The Word

> *Mary (at the feet of Jesus) with all the love of her heart, beheld the supreme wisdom of his Godhead wrapped in the mysterious words of his manhood. From this occupation she would not budge on account of anything she saw, heard spoken or done, about her. But she sat completely still in body and with many a sweet desire and delighted love pressed upon that high cloud of unknowing between her and her God . . . Mary was occupied in this cloud, sending forth her secret movements of love. Why? Because this is the highest and holiest state of contemplation we can have in this life* (The Cloud 17).

It is quite possible that here we have a clear illusion to the three phases of mystical love described by St Bernard. The first stage centres on the humanity of Jesus; Mary was at the feet of Christ. This must always be the beginning of our prayer. In the second phase the mind is occupied with the teachings of the faith concerning Christ; and in the final stage prayer is centered on the mystery of the Godhead. Thus Christ is both the beginning and also the end. Mary was totally absorbed in the mystery of God which she had come to know through the humanity of Christ. According to our author's understanding of the incident, recounted in St Luke's gospel (Lk 10:38-43), Mary was so absorbed that she did not hear her sister Martha ask for help. Martha was a practical woman, concerned with getting a job done, and done well; and she was obviously motivated by a deep love for Christ. But to her, Mary must have appeared at best forgetful, or at worst lazy. Such a thought can, indeed, strike the one who enters this form of prayer. We like to be active, or at least pass the test of being 'useful'. Sometimes contemplative prayer can seem like a sheer waste of time and opportunity; perhaps we feel we should be 'saying' our prayers, or at least 'thinking' godly thoughts. And St John of the Cross reassures us when he says that this prayer can indeed seem like 'doing nothing':

> If this inactivity should be a cause of scruples, remember that it is not a slight matter to possess our soul in peace and rest, without effect or desire. This is what our Lord requires at our hands, saying 'Be still, and see that I am God' (Ps 14:11). Learn to be interiorly empty of all things and you will see with delight that I am God
> *(Ascent of Mount Carmel II, 15, 3).*

Abbot Chapman addresses our hesitations in a very direct manner indeed:

> The time of prayer is passed by beginners in the act of *wanting God*. It is an idiotic state, and feels like a complete waste of time, until, gradually, it becomes more vivid *(Spiritual Letters pp 118-119).*

He reassures us that when we are still, quiet and speechless before God, we are still really at prayer, and wanting God. He suggests:

> It is much better to remain with God, apparently doing nothing in particular, than to make the grandest and most elaborate Meditations *(Spiritual Letters p 185).*

With his typical good humour the late Mgr. Ronald Knox once called this 'the prayer of stupidity'; we seem to be doing little or nothing. That can often be an embarrassment for people. For instance people who have to speak in public often find it difficult to know what to do with their hands when they are not busy with something. The same is true of our whole selves! Most of us have an urge to be fussing or fidgeting — or else feeling rather stupid. But reliable writers assure us that this is a quite legitimate stance in prayer: to still our volatile thoughts and restless bodies and simply *be* with God; and in some general, even if vague and ill-defined way, to *want* God. But, of course, it still seems like 'doing nothing in particular' and 'feels like a complete waste of time' as John Chapman says. And in one important sense it is 'doing nothing'.

It is quite true that we seek to direct all our attention towards 'wanting God'; we seek to make ourselves an open space, or a desert, or even retreat to our 'inner room' (there are numerous images we might employ). But when we have said all that we are still talking in terms of what *we* do and how *we* might do it. The more basic truth is that we are leaving ourselves open, fallow and receptive to what *God* is doing. In this matter especially 'There is no doer but He' as Julian tells us (*Revelations II*). And that is a mystery we cannot unravel, and about which we can only snatch hints and suggestions. So we seek to let God act; prayer is both 'what I do' and also 'what God does'. But in contemplative prayer we seek to grow less and less and leave God to grow more and more in us. It is not so much that we are totally passive, rather we very simply and deliberately give ourselves to God that he might work in us.

Thus we seek to direct our loving attention towards God; we seek to want him and to love him though we do not necessarily formulate those desires in so many words. We might well feel that this prayerful attitude is not one that we can maintain for very long. And our author reassures us on that score:

> This work does not require a long time to be truly done, as some people think, for it is the shortest work of all

that you can imagine. It is neither longer nor shorter than an atom. And an atom, according to the definition of reliable philosophers in the science of astrology, is the smallest particle of time. It is indeed so tiny that it is indivisible and nearly incomprehensible. But this is the time of which it is written: 'All time is given to you, and it shall be asked of you how you have spent it.' And it is a reasonable thing that you should give an account of it: for it is neither longer nor shorter but is exactly equivalent to one single stirring of the chief power of your soul, namely your will *(The Cloud 4)*.

Thus this prayer can be very brief indeed. We realise this the more when we take into account that according to medieval reckoning there were 22,560 'atoms' in an hour! Thus we do not have to think of being in this state of prayer for long periods, though the length will surely vary with circumstances and according to the grace given. Lord Michael Ramsay was once asked how long he spent each day in prayer, and he replied 'Two minutes — but I spend an hour preparing'. Doubtless he was speaking of prayer such as this.

Sometimes this intense longing for God to the exclusion of all else, can come during the time of prayer. Abbot Chapman speaks of 'ligature' — a break in the ordinary flow of prayer when it becomes impossible to attend to godly thoughts or 'say' or 'think' prayers in the sense of a conversation with God. Then, for however short or long a time possible, it is good to be simply quiet and be 'with God'. It is always a good indication of friendship if we can be with someone and not feel that we have to maintain an endless prattle of conversation.

But as to its length, this prayer can be long or short; it is not something that can be adequately measured by time. It is a matter of love and it pertains to eternity. These moments of prayer can indeed come at any time, and quite take us by surprise. As our author says:

> The perfection of this work is its suddenness, coming without any intervening means *(Epistle of Prayer)*.

So in all of this there is no hard and fast rule. With the freedom of the Spirit who blows where and when he wills, we must follow the prompting of grace:

> Be quite sure of this ... though I am saying that you ought to put yourself to this task simply and boldly, nevertheless I truly believe without any error or doubt that Almighty God, through his grace, is always the chief instigator and worker; whether he makes use of some method or not. And you, and any other like you, must simply consent and accept. However your consent and your acceptance must be such that in the time of this work, you are actively and readily given to this work in purity of spirit ... *(Privy Counsel 7)*.

Here again we see the author's delicate sensitivity to the mystery of grace. We are 'recipients', but active recipients. We do well to remember that prayer is taught by God; from what others have said we can be reassured that we are not deluding ourselves in prayer. Others have walked this path before us. We can place ourselves in God's hands. But we are not totally passive before the grace of God, but willing cooperators with it. As John Chapman says 'A contemplative must never be *resigned* to God's will, but must *will* it' *(Spiritual Letters p 122)*.

As we seek to 'will' the will of God in this matter, the author has a very practical hint for us. In order to unify ourselves, as it were, and direct our whole being to God, he suggests the use of a single word. This becomes a 'focus' for the whole of our prayer; it reduces our scattered thoughts and aspirations to one single point and faces us squarely in the direction of God. We seek to have a 'naked intention' directed to God alone:

> If you wish you may have this intention wrapped and enfolded in a single word. So as to have a better hold

> on it, take a little word of one syllable rather than two, for the shorter it is the better it accords with the working of the Spirit. Such a word is GOD or LOVE. Choose which one you prefer, or any other according to your liking — but of one syllable. Fasten this word to your heart so that it remains there whatever happens. This word shall be your shield and your spear, whether you are riding in peace or in war. With this word you are to beat on this cloud and this darkness above you
> *(The Cloud 7).*

The very idea of the use of a simple word suggests something about our prayer. It is being gradually simplified until we just 'want God and not any of his goods'. As we simplify our desiring, so also our scattered parts are being brought into a unity. But we must not think of the use of this word as some psychological gimmick we adopt to ensure that our attention is fixed on God. Certainly the use of this word will have something of that about it. But it is more than a handy learning device or a ruse that can rivet our attention on God. The word we choose is rather a compact summary of the Word of God. And that word we know is:

> living and active, sharper than any two-edged sword, piercing to the division of soul and spirit, of joints and marrow, and discerning the thoughts and intentions of the heart *(Heb 4:12).*

There is an incisive power about the Word that enables it to go straight to the essentials: to 'discern the thoughts and intentions of the heart'. The word of God is able to articulate those deepest longings which we can hardly stammer or stutter. In this prayer we take the word of God and make it our own in the deepest sense possible. We fix it on our heart; let it pierce to the very centre of our being. Or, to use the image of the prophet Jeremiah, we take the word and eat it and it becomes a joy to the heart (Jer 15:16). And such a word of God is not merely a sound or the sign of some idea, but it is a power, a growing conviction and indeed the very presence of the Holy Spirit (1 Thess 1:5).

Our author also suggests that we might use the word 'SIN' in this context also, for that word too, sums up our whole aspiration:

> Properly speaking prayer is nothing other than a devout intention directed unto God for the getting of good and the removal of evil. So, all evil is included in ... that little word 'sin'. And if we pray intently for the getting of good, let us cry with either word, thought, or desire, only the word 'God' *(The Cloud 39)*.

The whole of the gospel is summed up in either of these words. We are sinners, in need of healing; we are children of God longing for his Kingdom. In either word ('God' or 'sin') we focus on what we are: we adopt a radical realism. There is a certain urgency about the use of such a word. Once again we are reminded that our author is not encouraging us to indulge in any cosy occupation in prayer; we are actively involved in the great mystery of creation and redemption. Prayer is not a time of self indulgence, it is an active cooperation with the One whom Julian called 'Maker, Keeper and Lover' (*Revelations 4*). So our deepest longing is to be liberated from sin and united to God. Our prayer expresses an urgency. So our author tells us that when we are in some danger or deep personal need we cry for help. We do not indulge in long speeches, but we go straight to the essentials and seek to arouse attention and attract help:

> Yes. And how? Surely not in many words, nor even in one word of two syllables. And why is that? For you think it would be a waste of time to declare your urgent need and your anxiety. So you burst out in terror with one little word of a single syllable 'Fire' or perhaps 'Help' *(The Cloud 37)*.

And he reminds us that this is not some intellectual exercise. Here we are in touch with a power quite beyond our own powers:

> Do not analyse or expound these words in an attitude of intellectual curiosity, as if such a procedure would increase your devotion. I believe that it will not be so in the case of this work. But take these words as they are: whole. By the word 'sin' mean an unspecified lump: nothing else, in fact, than your very self *(The Cloud 36)*.

So we are certainly being encouraged not to 'meditate' in the sense of prolonged thoughts; and certainly we are not to indulge in some elaborate self-analysis or examination of conscience. We just take the simple fact that we are sinful and need God. The 'unspecified lump' is the recognition and acceptance of this sinfulness and this need for God. We do not delve further, we turn ourselves to God. Through this small word 'sin' the Holy Spirit is teaching us the truth about ourselves; and by the gift of the same Spirit we are being cleansed, and through the love which the Spirit is pouring into our hearts we are enabled to love God. Thus this 'word' becomes less a mere word we employ and more 'the word' which becomes what all true prayer is 'God's breath in man returning to its birth' (George Herbert, *Prayer*). Here God is the teacher, God is the doer, God is the one who prays in us:

> This spiritual cry is better taught by God through experience rather than by the word of another. It is best when it is pure spirit, when there is no particular thought of word pronounced, though occasionally because of the fullness of spirit, it can burst into words; for both body and soul are filled with sorrow and the weight of sin *(The Cloud 40)*.

13. Forgetting

> *Lift up your heart to God with a meek stirring of love and mean God himself and none of his goods. And so be loath to think of anything but God himself, so that nothing occupies your mind or will but only God. Do everything possible to forget all the creatures that God has ever made and all their works, so that your thoughts or desires are not directed or stretched to any of them either in general or particular. Let them be; pay no heed to them. This is the work of the soul that pleases God most* (The Cloud 3).

Our author's first mention of the 'cloud of unknowing' is linked with his introduction of the idea of the 'cloud of forgetting'. Not merely must we direct our loving attention on God but at the same time we must turn away from creatures; this is a practical application of the basic couplet of the spiritual life: we must turn away from evil and do good. It is merely good, sound commonsense that if we have a particular aim in view, then that aim should preclude other interests and pursuits: to pilot a jumbo jet or bake a cake requires some degree of concentration and attention that must necessarily mean some turning away from other occupations.

There is a long tradition of Christian practice which helps this 'turning aside' from other interests during prayer. Generally people have practiced a minimal asceticism regarding bodily posture, and closing one's eyes has been an obvious effort to 'blanket out' surrounding sights that might prove a distraction to prayer.

The poet John Donne captures the Christian attitude in 'A Hymne to Christ':

> Seale then this bill of my Divorce to All,
> On whom those fainter beames of love did fall;
> Marry those loves, which in youth scattered bee
> On Fame, Wit, Hopes (false mistresses) to thee.
> Churches are best for Prayer, that have least light
> To see God only, I goe out of sight;
> And to scape stormy dayes, I chuse
> An Everlasting night.

If we are to attend to God, we must separate ourselves from all else that claims our love and affection. This amounts to a 'divorce' from all such things, and especially from our own personal ambitions. We can be 'scattered' by running after these 'false mistresses'. So we willingly accept some darkness, some night, in order that we might 'see God only'. This, of course, means taking up our cross. And in the *Privy Counsel* our author several times adverts to the fact that we are a cross for ourselves.

For this desire to accept a 'divorce' from all, means a real sharing in the cross of Christ. Without such a Christian asceticism we cannot come to this life of deep intimate love with God which we call contemplation. The idea of a cross accepted, a severance endured, a turning one's back on attachments, form a necessary stage in the growth of this 'love affair' with God. In this context spiritual writers often use the words of Psalm 45:

> Hear, O daughter, consider and incline your ear;
> Forget your people and your Father's house
> *(Ps 45:10).*

And indeed, this love affair a Christian would have with God, is often likened to a marriage. This necessarily involves some turning away from old loyalties and familiar places. Commenting on this text Walter Hilton places this image firmly in the context of turning away from sin and cleaving to God:

> Here you may see how our Lord calls you and all others who will listen to him. What hinders you then, that you can neither see him nor hear him? Indeed, there is so much din and disturbance in your heart arising from foolish thoughts and bodily desires ... put away all this restless noise, and break your love of sin and vanity ... *(Ladder of Perfection I, 50)*.

The Psalm, on which Hilton is commenting, is speaking of a betrothal. Hence the idea is reinforced by the image taken from Donne: there must be a divorce from all else, if our love for God is to be genuine. Our author reiterates this message with great emphasis:

> If ever you come to this cloud, and live and work in it as I bid you, just as the cloud of unknowing is above you, between you and your God, so you must also put a cloud of forgetting beneath you; that is between you and all the creatures that have ever been made. It seems to you, perhaps, that you are very far from God because of this cloud of unknowing between you and your God. But surely, it would be more correct to say that you are much further from him when you have no cloud of forgetting between you and all creatures that have ever been made. Whenever I say 'all creatures that have ever been made' I mean not merely the creatures themselves, but also all their works and circumstances ... In short, I say that all creatures should be hid under this cloud of forgetting *(The Cloud 5)*.

In this sort of prayer any thought of anything at all is a 'distancing' of oneself from God. We can be 'scattered' over a wide variety of interests and aims. In so far as we attend to them, we are concentrating more on them than on God. And our author goes on to say that this is simply a matter of common sense. This is a practical decision to have a singleness of aim; just as 'the eye of the bowman is fixed upon the target he is shooting at' (*The Cloud 5*). In this image he reiterates the teaching of John Cassian (d 435):

> When expert archers want to display their prowess ... they try to shoot their arrows into little targets which have the prizes painted on them: they know that they can only win the prize which is their real goal by shooting straight into the mark which is their immediate goal
> *(Conferences I, 5).*

So in this prayer, we must rivet our loving gaze on God to the exclusion of all else. If we let something else occupy our attention then that 'something else' can be truly said to dominate us:

> Everything you think about is 'above you' while you think about it, and it is between you and your God. Insofar as there is anything in your mind except God alone, then thus far are you further from God *(The Cloud 5).*

So far this teaching merely reiterates the need to make our clear choices in life. We can be enticed by numerous attractions and be swayed by a complexity of desires. At some stage we need to make our clear choices and as people of faith have our definite priorities in life. But in speaking of contemplation the author pushes his argument further. He doubtless startles the reader by pushing this teaching so far as to say:

> If I may say so in a courteous and seemly manner, in this work it profits you little or nothing to think of the kindness or the worthiness of God, or of our Lady or the saints or angels in heaven, or even the joys of heaven. That is to say with a special attention to them as if by so doing you might feed and strengthen your purpose.

> I believe that in no wise would it help you in this particular matter. For although it is good to think of the kindness of God and to love him and praise him for it, it is far better to think about him as he is and to love and praise him for himself *(The Cloud 5)*.

It is important to note that he quite clearly stresses that it 'is a good thing to think of the kindness of God' and other such thoughts that can be the subject of our prayer. Time and again he mentions the need for 'meditation', or thinking through aspects of our faith. But here he is insistent: 'it is better to think about (God) as he is', that is, as the fundamental mystery we cannot adequately conceive. Hence we face the ultimate darkness that must confront us when we stand before the majesty of God: all words have proved inadequate and all sounds hollow; all images have been rendered futile and all colour wanting. But as we have seen this is not a void, or a merely frustrating negation. It at once points to the very greatness of God and also the insufficiency of our feeble efforts to appreciate him. Here such 'meditations', thoughts and words that we might legitimately use betimes simply do not 'strengthen (our) purpose', they merely degenerate into pious prattle when a deeply reverent and loving silence is more appropriate.

And so, according to our author, we are propelled into an argument within ourselves. We have to argue ourselves out of the habit of trying to comprehend things, asking 'why?' and then neatly placing matters within measurable bounds and neat categories. We must learn to live with mystery:

> If your mind asks you 'what is that God?' Reply that it is the God who made you, ransomed you and graciously called you to his love. And furthermore say 'you have no part to play'. So say to such a thought 'you have no skill in these matters' and therefore insist 'Get down',

and tread it down quickly with a stirring of love, even though it seems a genuinely holy thought such as would help you seek God. Perhaps the thought will bring to your mind a variety of lovely and wonderful points of God's kindness, and remind you of God's sweetness and love, his graciousness and mercy. If you will listen to him, such a thought asks no more. For eventually it will chatter incessantly until it brings you down to think of Christ's passion. There it will let you see the wonderful kindness of God: and it wants nothing better than that you pay heed. For soon after that it will let you see your former wretched manner of living, and as you see it and think of it, it will bring to mind some place where you used to live. The result is that, before you are even aware of it, you will be scattered beyond belief ... Nevertheless such thoughts are both good and holy. So holy indeed that no one should desire to come to contemplation without prior and many sweet meditations: on your own wretchedness, the Passion, the kindness and great goodness and worthiness of God. Otherwise you will surely err and fail in your purpose. At the same time, if you are long practised in such meditations, leave them aside and put them down and hold them far down under the cloud of forgetting if you are ever to pierce the cloud of unknowing between you and your God *(The Cloud 7)*.

Again he returns to his favorite tripartite description of God as the one who creates, ransoms and calls to prayer. His stress is always on what God *does*. After that we simply and firmly tell our reasoning powers that they have no further part to play. And with great skill and gentle humour he shows us how easy it is for the holiest of thoughts to be but the beginning of a road that leads to our favorite topic — self. He takes great pains to ensure that we understand that we must at times have a 'thought-prayer' or meditation; that is the necessary prerequisite for contemplation; but it is also true that it outlives its purpose; we can only go so far along the road of understanding and talking. We need to face the possibility that we are called to go by a different path. For in contemplation we seek to stand before the mystery of God and also to be liberated from all manner of self-searching; introspection; or selfishness by whatever name.

And here he challenges us to see the very essence of our self-interest: self-interest is, at its worst, unredeemed nature. It is pictured for us in the scriptures in the character of the Prodigal who says 'Give me . . .' in a spirit of self-interest that involves a turning away from father, family and home — from the deepest of commitments to others. In our time of prayer we can all too easily indulge in a form of self-seeking. We can find ourselves rehearsing old battles, reopening old wounds, and indulging in all manner of complaints, criticisms and animosities. So many of these things can cling to the heart, and indeed can eat into our hearts as a cancer. So he warns:

> But if you permit some interest or complaint to be fastened to the surface of your heart unreproved for some time, then in the end it will be fastened to the depths of your heart (that is to say your will). If this is done with full consent then it is a deadly sin. And this happens when you wilfully call to mind any living man or woman or indeed any bodily or worldly thing. If it is something which grieves you now or has grieved you previously, and you experience a rising passionate anger and an appetite for revenge — then it is *wrath*. Or if you despise and loath such persons with spiteful and harsh thoughts — it is *envy*. Or if you experience a listless weariness for any good physical or spiritual occupation — that is *sloth*
> *(The Cloud 10).*

This is a particularly powerful analysis of that deeply embedded selfishness which we call sin. However religious our thoughts, words and aspirations might be, the sinful self is not far from the surface. What medievalists liked to categorise as the seven deadly sins lurk in the shallows, ready to surprise us. And we all know how easy it is to allow the mind to wander down the path of memories and soon stumble over past hurts, wrongs (real or imaginary), hostilities only thinly disguised by perfunctory courtesies.

Doubtless the human memory has powerful abilities to recall. We can 're-live' a particular incident and clothe it in all the hues and colours which make it a realistic scene. But more than that, we can also re-call a particular emotional attitude from the past. Doubtless these powers can exercise a dramatic influence on us years after an event. Perhaps a number of these might be harmless enough in themselves; though we always run the danger of regressing into a romanticised or overly sentimental view of our own past. And the ability to recall emotional involvements can be dangerous and destructive. It is always sad to encounter people struggling through life with the accumulated emotional lumber of the past; ever ready to rekindle the fire of old animosities and passions. In contemplation we subject the memory to a severe pruning. To divest ourselves of so much of the past can be a significant aspect of personal liberation. Conversely, to give memories full scope can end in a real enslavement. Hence our author warns:

> And therefore the intense activity of your mind, which will always press upon you when you set yourself to this blind work, must be put down. For if you do not suppress it, it will suppress you! Often when you imagine that you can best abide in this darkness, and that there is nothing in your mind but only God, when you examine carefully you will find that your mind is not occupied with this darkness, but with a clear picture of something less than God. And if this is so, surely that thing is temporarily on top of you, and between you and your God
> *(The Cloud 9).*

The power of memory and imagination are such that they can speedily draw us into the vortex of self-analysis and self-concern. It is not too much to say, with our author, that they are often 'on top of' us. St Theodoros (9th century) says 'memories of all the impassioned actions we have performed exert an impassioned tyranny over the soul' (*Philokalia II, 16*). And here, something of our real selves is being unmasked; our real self is being revealed to ourselves. Such memories reveal something of the human heart. So we do well to ponder the gospel warning:

> what proceeds from the heart ... defiles a person. For out of the heart come evil thoughts, murder, adultery, fornication, theft, false witness, slander *(Mt 14:18-19)*.

So we seek to be docile to the work of the Spirit and leave ourselves open to his softening and humanizing influence:

> do not harden your hearts
> as in the rebellion
> on the day of testing in the wilderness
> *(Heb 3:8)*.

Indeed the wilderness enables all manner of rebellious thoughts to come to the surface. This is one way in which our prayer resembles that of the Desert Fathers. They went into the wilderness after the manner of the Baptist and indeed the Lord himself. There, in that arid terrain, they were divorced from the customary elements of life. In the desert the human being has little to lean on for support. The wilderness leaves us vulnerable and a prey to conflict and attack. The desert is the place of struggle between good and evil, a pitched battle takes place. And where do we turn for help? The Holy Spirit comes to our aid and prays within us. As we have seen, that little word — God or Sin — sums up the whole gospel. That little word is, in effect, the Word of God in the form of a telegram.

Through that Word we seek victory. It alone is sufficient for the conflict: it is 'the helmet of salvation, and the sword of the Spirit' (Eph 6:17). So our author advises us to use this little word of one syllable which he has advised before. As we shall see, this radical act of 'forgetting' is in order that we might be healed; re-membered, made whole.

14. Re-membering

> *With this word you shall smite down all manner of thought under the cloud of forgetting. So much so that if any thought presses itself upon your attention asking what you are seeking, this one word shall be sufficient answer for you. And if the thought offers you, out of its great learning, to analyze that word for you and to tell you its meaning, reply that you prefer to have the word whole, not taken apart and explained . . .*
> (The Cloud 7).

This is not the time for speculation or linguistic games. By the word 'Sin' we sum up the thraldom from which we would be liberated; while the word 'God' calls upon the one who alone can give us the freedom he wills for his children. But we do not use the word with any great clarity of meaning, or think of specific attitudes when we use it. As Abbot Chapman says:

> the soul means *so much more than the words say*, that the words are rather suggestions than expressions *(Spiritual Letters p 136).*

The Spirit is interceding for us with 'sighs too deep for words' (Rom 8:26). And as the Spirit prays in us we are not engaging in some 'cover-up' exercise; we are not simply sweeping unpleasant memories under the rug of 'forgetting'. We are in fact being enabled to let go, to strip away part of ourselves; and this amounts to a healing process. The forgetting involves a surrender of self, a 'self-emptying'; this is being done in the power of the Spirit and as such is also a radical healing of self. The heart of stone is being taken from us and we are being given a heart of flesh: becoming what we should be as children of God made in his image and likeness. This is a painful process, a real dying: we are, as our author says 'a cross to yourself' (*Privy Counsel 8*):

> also in this work you must forget both yourself and also your deeds done for God, and also all other creatures and their deeds *(The Cloud 33)*.

This 'forgetting' is even a complete renunciation of self:

> But now you will ask me how you may destroy this naked awareness and experience of your own existence. For doubtless you think that if this could be destroyed, all other hindrances would thereby be destroyed. If you think so, you are certainly right! To this I answer that without a special grace (fully and) freely given by God, and a corresponding capacity on your part to receive this grace, the naked awareness and experience of your own existence can in no way be destroyed. And this capacity is nothing else but a strong and deep spiritual sorrow!
>
> But in such sorrow you need to have discretion: be wary in such a time of sorrow that you do not too vigorously strain your body or your spirit. Rather sit very still as though you were in a deep sleep, absorbed and sunk in sorrow *(The Cloud 44)*.

Our author sees this complete forgetfulness of self as synonymous with a 'strong and deep sorrow'. Here we have lost our lives that we might find them, and this is the work of the Spirit within us. This is not something we can 'force' or 'engender' by some technique: we have a growing peace and stillness, and these are hints of the presence of God himself.

We must take this teaching in the context of the author's insistence on our fidelity to the ministry of the Church in the matter of reconciliation (see chapter 5). But ecclesial and sacramental grace do not act without personal involvement. Here, in this prayer, we seek to move away from our self interest and concern and leave ourselves at the disposal of God's healing Word. We allow that Word full scope in our hearts. The emphasis is increasingly on what the Spirit does within us. But it is still 'our' work. On numerous occasions the author describes this prayer as 'work': in *The Cloud 26*, for instance, he uses the word 'trauaile' (= labour, the verb) once; 'trauayle' (the noun) 10 times, and the word 'werk' six times in describing aspects of forgetting. The consistent teaching of the Fathers is that we have here a real asceticism. Evagrios Pontikos (345-399) sums up a great Christian tradition when he advises:

> When you pray, keep close watch on your memory, so that it does not distract you with recollections of your past. But make yourself aware that you are standing before God. For by nature the intellect is apt to be carried away by memories during prayer *(The Philokalia I, 61)*.

And this is especially the case when the memory tends to harken back to former sins. St Maximos the Confessor (580-662), as always, combines a great practical sense with his theological insights when he warns:

> Just as it is easier to sin in the mind than in action, so warfare through our impassioned conceptual images of things is harder than warfare through things themselves *(Philokalia II, 77)*.

The control of the memory and imagination are a real area of Christian asceticism and a 'death' to so much of self. It is little wonder that our author refers to this aspect of our prayer in terms such as 'work'. In addition such words are used several times in his description of 'forgetting' in chapter 26 where he outlines his teaching on this matter:

> But where is the hard work then? Surely this work is in the treading down of the remembrance of all the creatures that God ever made, and holding them under the cloud of forgetting, already spoken of. For this is all labour; this is our work, helped by God's grace. And the other, that is to say the stirring of love, that is the work of God alone. So do your part in this work, and I promise he will not fail you *(The Cloud 26)*.

Again we see the author's ability to steer between Scylla and Charybdis; making due allowance for the mystery of grace and free will at work in the individual Christian. But he is equally sure that the 'stirring of love' which is the heart of this prayer is nothing other than God himself, the love of God being poured into our hearts, the Spirit praying in us. And so the work which is so difficult at first and for a time, eventually becomes easier:

> For although this is difficult and restricting in the beginning when you have no devotion, nevertheless, after a time, when devotion has come, it shall become very restful and easy for you, though it was so hard before. Then you shall have very little labour, or indeed none at all. For God will work sometimes all by himself, but not all the time, or even for a long time, but just when he likes and as he likes. Then you will be delighted to let him have his own way *(The Cloud 26)*.

Perhaps the great difficulty in all this matter of forgetting is that central to the Christian life is an act of remembering. The Lord took bread, blessed it, broke it, gave thanks, and gave it to his disciples saying 'do this in memory of me'. And here we are being asked to forget all manner of things. Not just the evil and destructive (which is surely a good thing to do) but also the good and the beautiful and even the sacred; and we are asked to forget ourselves as well. But the difficulty is more apparent than real. While capable of much destruction, the memory is one of our most hope-filled faculties pointing to our eventual transfiguration.

Perhaps our memories will be granted the freedom to gather our whole selves, not merely as a succession of events and experiences but as an ever-present NOW. But to do that they need to be redeemed. And here there must be a great harmony between our personal prayer and the great act of remembering: Christ has died, Christ is risen, Christ will come again! The very drama of the liturgy brings together past present and future. We celebrate the one who emptied himself and who has risen and is our life. We too must follow him and make personal this act of self-emptying that we might be filled with his risen life. In contemplation we simply make our own what the liturgy enables us to do: empty ourselves, lose our lives, die to sin, that we might be alive in Christ. Forgetting is nothing more than making our own the 'death' we all must undergo in order to be re-membered, made whole.

15. Growth

> *Then God will sometimes send out a beam of spiritual light piercing this cloud of unknowing between you and him, and reveal something of his ultimate self. Concerning this spiritual light human beings may not and cannot speak. Then you shall feel your affection aflame with the fire of his love, far more than I can tell you or indeed may or wish to at this time. For that work, which is God's business, I will not dare to speak with my blabbing human tongue. If I dared to speak I would not do so. But I am very pleased to speak of the human aspect of this work, when you feel yourself stirred and helped by grace; that is the less hazardous matter to discuss*
> (The Cloud 26).

Considering the author's insistence that the 'cloud of unknowing' is always between us and our God, the nature of this 'spiritual light' revealing something of God's 'intimate self' is not immediately clear. So this repeated stress on God as the mystery which can only be known through his work suggests that this spiritual light will most probably be a deeper 'awareness of', a more complete confidence in, the God who though 'unknown' is all the while creating, redeeming and calling us in love. This surely is the nature of faith — to persevere in the darkness, yet be ever more confidently committed to the God who does great things for us. It is not a matter of having some visual experience or indeed of 'seeing' in some intellectual fashion. But the author clearly posits the possibility of some special experience.

Walter Hilton uses similar language. He speaks of the spiritual life as a journey to Jerusalem and the Christian as one who seeks to have his heart set on this goal. Such a Christian will be encouraged by a special grace:

> And by the time this takes place you are fast nearing Jerusalem. You have not yet reached it, but you will be able to see the city in the distance before you come to it because of the twinkling rays of light shining from it. For remember that although your soul dwells in this peaceful darkness, untroubled by thoughts of the world, it is not yet at the end of its journey, for it is not yet clothed in light or wholly ablaze with the fire of love. It is fully conscious of something beyond itself which as yet it neither knows or possesses, but has an ardent longing for *(The Ladder of Perfection II 25)*.

But this is not some unusual phenomenon. The grace is not some 'sight' of God in any literal sense. Hilton explains:

> As I understand it, this knowledge of Jesus is the opening of heaven to the eyes of a pure soul of which the saints speak in their writings. But this opening of heaven does not imply, as some imagine, that the soul can see in imagination our Lord Jesus sitting in His majesty in a visible light as brilliant as that of a hundred suns. This is not so, for however high man's vision may penetrate, he cannot see the heaven of heavens. Indeed, the higher he aspires beyond the sun in his imagination, the lower he falls beneath it. Notwithstanding, thinking of our Lord in this way is permissible for simple souls, who know no better way of seeking Him who is invisible
> *(The Ladder of Perfection II 32)*.

This accords well with St Peter's appreciation of the experience on the mount of transfiguration. What was significant for him was not the experience itself, though at the time he wanted it to be permanent (Mt 17:4), but the deepening of faith:

we were with him on the holy mountain. And we had the prophetic word made more sure. This (is) a lamp shining in a dark place *(2 Pt 1:18-19)*.

However the author would seem to leave the possibility open for some indescribable experience. This is reminiscent of St Paul's account of his own mystical experience:

> ... this man was caught up into paradise — whether in the body or out of the body I do not know, God knows — and he heard things that cannot be told, which man may not utter *(2 Cor 12:3-4)*.

But this is not the norm. Our author clearly does not want to attempt any description of such experiences; he sees no point in displaying interest in the extraordinary. The section quoted above from *The Cloud 26* comes immediately after the vigorous description of the effort involved in the 'cloud of forgetting'. There, the person of prayer is required to display strength, discipline and self-denial amounting to hard work. But the cross which is involved in all of this is soon followed by some beams of resurrection light: at least we experience some peace, some growing confidence, some deeper awareness of the reality of God.

Yet when we speak of 'growth' in relation to prayer, we must be very clear that such experiences are not infallible signs of true growth. And we must be equally sure that these experiences ought not be sought for their own sake. We do not pray in order to have a pleasing sense of confidence, or a tangible awareness of peace. This work is a search for God and not any of his gifts, as our author so emphatically states. Indeed he is not concerned to delineate any specific details of the growth we experience in prayer: he is merely sure that such growth does take place.

Prayer is not a static thing. Neither is it a self quest in which we seek to engender certain 'states' and 'experiences'.

We do not take overly much notice of our inner feelings or insights. The cloud of forgetting involves a radical forgetting of self. We blanket our self-analysis, and steer clear of anything that might smack of 'religious experience' for its own sake. And while our author says that 'ravishing' or 'rapture' is the 'perfection of this work' (*The Cloud 71*) he gives us no details about this at all. What many people regard as the 'higher states' of prayer interest him very little. So, as we have seen, he has little interest in ecstasy, though he recognises that such a state is possible. On the other hand the whole tenor of the author's works is that such are not essential aspects of contemplative prayer. The 'ordinary' committed Christian can practise this form of prayer and bear the fruit of this grace. Indeed states such as ecstasy might well simply be passing phases occasioned by the human inability to bear the weight of God's glory.

In Catholic tradition there is a healthy suspicion about such occurrences. St Paul was given a 'thorn ... in the flesh' to prevent his placing too much emphasis on extraordinary states. And our author clearly does not place too much emphasis on them either. Indeed he turns the full blast of his humour on those who would aspire to something akin to a 'mystical' posture. He has little patience with people who

> stare as though they were mad, and look as though they saw the devil. It is just as well they are wary for indeed the fiend is not far away! Some set their eyes in their heads as though they were mad sheep beaten across the head and about to expire. Some hang their heads on one side as if a worm were in their ears. Some squeak instead of speaking as if there were no spirit in their bodies ...
> *(The Cloud 53)*

This surely takes us back to what is implied in our commitment to Christ (Chapter 2). To be a friend of Christ and walk with him as companion and saviour is to be 'ordinary', simply human, and at the same time to be at ease with mystery. Growth is not to be measured by the bizarre and the unusual: rather growth implies so deep a commitment to the ordinary and the simple as to find in them the presence of the divine. But can our growth be measured in terms of our feelings about such things? Do these indicate a growth in prayer and a sensitivity to the mystery that pervades all? Our author is very clear that feelings are not of the essence of contemplation:

> We should direct all our attention on this meek stirring of love in our will. As regards all other sweetness and comfort, either physical or spiritual, however likeable or holy (if it be courteous and seemly to say so), we should have a certain recklessness. If they come, welcome them: but don't depend overly much on them through a fear of weakness. For it will tax your powers too much if you stay with such sweet feelings and tears for any length of time. It could well happen that you may be moved to love God for the sake of having them. You will be able to tell whether this is so, if you grumble unduly when they are withdrawn *(The Cloud 50)*.

So we are brought back to a central principle in this work: we must seek God and not any of his gifts *(The Cloud 3)*. It is all too easy to like prayer when it is pleasant; to judge prayer to have been successful and satisfactory when we find ourselves aglow with fervour; to have a tangible sensation of the aptness of our prayer; or indeed to feel a compelling enthusiasm for the things of God and for doing good deeds. Our author is quite prepared to take all this when it comes: but not to see it as essential, and indeed to be equally content when we are dry and unmoved in our prayer. Certainly we must not pray in order to seek any such 'feelings'. At the end of *The Book of Privy Counsel* he places such emotional responses in context. God can give these feelings; and he can (and does) remove them:

> By withdrawing this fervour (in which case you think he has departed but this is not so) he is really testing your patience. For be very clear about this: God sometimes withdraws this feeling of sweetness, these fervent feelings and these burning desires. Nevertheless he never withdraws his grace from his chosen ones. For I truly believe that his special grace will never be withdrawn from his chosen ones that have been touched by it, unless mortal sin be the cause *(Privy Counsel 12)*.

Thus a variety of 'feelings' can be given and might well prove helpful. But they are not signs of growth. Indeed real growth might be indicated by their absence. After the section just quoted he immediately proceeds to say:

> But all this felt sweetness; these fervent feelings and these burning desires are not themselves grace but merely the tokens of grace. They are often withdrawn to test our patience and oft times for other spiritual profit, more than we can ever guess. For grace itself is so pure, so spiritual, that it cannot be perceived by the senses *(Privy Counsel 12)*.

Here we move beyond the gifts of God to God himself; here the Christian is not merely concerned with his or her own 'comfort', or 'ease' or peace of mind. The individual has, as it were, 'stripped self of self' as the author advises. This is the death to self which is necessary if we are to experience the new life which Christ brings through his death and resurrection. And so in a very moving piece he sums up the love which can endure despite the absence of emotional supports and rewards.

> Now your love is both chaste and perfect. Now you both see your God and your love and nakedly feel him by the spiritual union with him in the highest point of your spirit. You experience him just as he is in himself, but blindly, as must needs be the case in this life. You are

now utterly stripped of yourself and nakedly clothed in himself as he is and not wrapped in any of those sensible feelings (be they ever so sweet and holy) that might come to you in this life. But in purity of spirit you may properly and perfectly perceive and feel him as he is in himself, far removed from any fantasy or false opinion that might be expected from this life *(Privy Counsel 12)*.

This is a very moving piece, quite sensuous in its language. Images from human love are used to clothe the author's teaching but once again he is not indulging in any gross literalism. He uses the language of sensual love to express what is above sensual love. Once again we are brought back to the following of Christ. This involves our being able to take the commonplace and the familiar and see them charged with a new power and beauty. The simple things of life become the symbols of God's presence and love and saving grace. It seems to be an invariable part of the divine plan that the more grossly physical and material things are the better able they are to be signs and instruments of the great mystery of God.

And this piece once again prompts us to move beyond the mere literal use of words and images. The author tells us that now we 'see' God and indeed 'feel' him. When we 'see' a thing we can be said to 'know' it: when a difficult mathematical problem has been explained the response 'I see' is not unusual. We now realise the truth. And similarly when we 'feel' something we have an awareness of its proximity and compelling power, even though our feelings can deceive and exaggerate. We say that we 'feel' happy or angry; or that we 'feel' a rough surface. When we use such language we mean that we are aware of our feelings; they are real to us; they exert a compelling influence over us. When we say we 'feel' God we are not using the term in any literal physical or emotional sense, though that gives us some hint and suggestion to work on. Rather we mean that we are sure of God, aware of his proximity, confident of his love. Now in this blind darkness which is 'as must needs be the case in this life' we can say with St Paul 'I know whom I have believed' (2 Tim 1:12).

Thus our author points to a profound personal relationship with God as the real sign of growth in prayer. There comes an abiding relationship with God which is not dependent upon the fair weather of pleasing emotions. The soul has been 'onyd to God in spirit' *(The Cloud 25)* as our author so often says. It is in the context of this relationship that growth takes place. This relationship with God is not a terminus; it is an interpersonal relationship in which human growth takes place. Indeed the God in whom we live and move and have our being is the very condition, the atmosphere or the 'place' in which our growth takes place. The contemplative is deeply in touch with the 'ground of our being' in which we can grow. But the God in whom we live is not merely the sum total of suitable conditions in which growth takes place. By the word 'God' we do not simply mean the assemblage of all that suits us, or profits us. The God in whom we believe is utterly simple. He is also profoundly personal. It is only through a deep personal communion with God that we grow. Thus it is little wonder that our author, in one of his most mature works, makes use of the image of marriage to describe this close personal relationship with God:

> According to the word of St Paul 'Qui adheret Deo, unus spiritus est cum illo' (1 Cor 6:17). That is to say: 'whoever draws near to God' as is the case in such a reverent affection which was discussed previously 'he is one spirit with God'. That is to say that although the human being and God are two, and distinct in nature, nevertheless they are so knit together that they become one spirit. And all this is so because of the unity of love and the harmony of will. And in this unity (there) is made the marriage between God and the soul which shall never be broken even though the heat and fervour of this work cease for

a time. It shall only be broken by mortal sin. In the spiritual experience of this unity a loving soul may both say and sing, if it so wishes, this holy word written in the *Song of Songs* in the bible: 'Dilectus meus mihi et ego illi'. That is to say: 'My beloved is mine and I am his'. By which it is understood 'shall be knit by grace (the goostly glewe of grace) on his part, and by the loving consent and joy of spirit on your part *(Epistle of Prayer)*.

In the bible marriage is an oft-recurring image of the relationship between God and the individual as well as between God and his people. In the opening chapters of Hosea, this marriage is clearly indicated though there is a glaring disparity in the worth of the partners

> And the Lord said to me, 'Go again, love a woman who is beloved of a paramour and is an adulteress; even as the Lord loves the people of Israel, though they turn to other gods . . .' *(Hos 3:1)*.

And our author is very clear that the marriage can break down through mortal sin on our part. But despite the disparity due to human frailty, the Spouse is Maker, Redeemer and Lover:

> For your Maker is your husband,
> the Lord of hosts is his name;
> and the Holy One of Israel is your Redeemer,
> the God of the whole earth he is called.
> For the Lord has called you
> like a wife forsaken and grieved in spirit,
> like a wife of youth when she is cast off,
> says your God.
> For a brief moment I forsook you,
> but with great compassion I will gather you
> *(Is 54:5-7)*.
>
> You shall no more be termed Forsaken,
> and your land shall no more be termed Desolate,
> but you shall be called My delight is in her,
> and your land Married;

> for the Lord delights in you,
> and your land shall be married.
> For as a young man marries a virgin,
> so shall your sons marry you,
> and as the bridegroom rejoices over the bride,
> so shall your God rejoice over you
> *(Is 62:4-5).*

Despite the rejection caused by sin, the Lord remains faithful. And this is a cause for joy. In the New Testament the kingdom of God is likened to a wedding feast (Mt 22:1-14). And we look forward to this with great expectancy for Christ clearly alludes to himself as the bridegroom eagerly awaited by the wise virgins (Mt 25:1-12). Then the presence of this bridegroom mitigates the need for fasting: this is cause for rejoicing (Mt 9:15).

This use of the marriage image to describe the relationship of God with the Christian is common in our tradition. Thus St Makarius of Egypt (300-390) shows how this involves a real sharing:

> When a woman comes to live and share her life with a man, all that each has is held in common. They share one house, a single being and existence ... Similarly the soul, in its true and ineffable communion with Christ, becomes one spirit with Him (1 Cor 6:17). It necessarily follows that, since the soul has become His bride, it is, as it were, mistress of all His untold treasures. For there is no doubt that, when God joined himself to the soul, all that He has belongs also to the soul, whether it would be world, life, death, angels, principalities, things present or things to come (Rom 8:38) *(Philokalia III, 340).*

And the same saint, makes the point that the purpose of Christ's coming is specifically 'the restoration and integration of human nature in Him', and that this is achieved by enabling the human being 'to become Christ's bride and consort through the communion of the Holy Spirit' *(Philokalia III, 353).*

However no Christian writer uses the marriage image more clearly and more elaborately than St Teresa of Avila in the *Interior Castle*. There, the marriage takes place at the end of a long search for the Lord who dwells in the inmost recess of the Castle. However, Teresa does not see it simply as some static terminus, coming at the end of a romantic search: the marriage between God and the human being is dynamic and productive. Nonetheless our author has a different emphasis: he does not see the marriage as being the culminating point. For him it is rather the framework in which the human growth takes place all along. Just as there are phases of growth in a human marriage, there are times when 'the heat and fervour ... cease for a time'. And of course this intimate relationship can be 'broken by mortal sin'. Of its very nature marriage has a relationship to the bearing of fruit. St Teresa is always clear about that:

> *This* is the end and aim of prayer, my daughters; *this* is the reason of the spiritual marriage whose children are always good works. *Works* are the unmistakable sign which shows these favours come from God ...
> *(Interior Castle VII, 4, 10).*

Part 3

You Will Know Them by Their Fruits (Mt 7:16)

16. Bearing Fruit

> *As I said at the beginning, climb up this tree and you (will) come to the fruit: that is (to this) reverent affection which always will be in you ... The longer the fruit is separated from the tree ... the sweeter it smells and the better it pleases the high king of Heaven; and when you feel sweetness and comfort in what you are doing, then he is breaking the fruit and giving you part of your own present*
> (Epistle of Prayer).

This is a sudden change of image on the part of the author; and it comes immediately after his description of marriage as an image of our relationship with God. In speaking of the tree, he is merely returning to the original image with which he began this short work. This is indeed a favourite concept with medieval writers. The tree (of prayer) must be well grounded in the soil of a reverent dread of God. This holy dread comes from realising our own frailty: and he brings this home to his disciple by reminding him that so fragile is he, that he could die before the end of his prayer. The trunk of the tree is the virtue of hope:

> what moves a life more fervently towards doing good than a sure hope in the mercy and goodness of God ... *(Epistle of Prayer)*?

This hope, he says, is a trunk 'sure and steady' and through this people are stirred to perform works of love; and 'these good works are the branches' *(Epistle of Prayer)*. But good works are done for others. The author quite clearly looks towards the separation of the fruit from the tree.

> As long as the fruit is still attached to the tree it has a little of the green smell of the tree. But when it has been separated from the tree and is fully ripe, then it has lost all the taste of the tree and is fit food for a king, whereas before it was but fit for menial servants *(Epistle of Prayer)*.

Here the author speaks of the fruit being separated and enjoyed.

In the previous section he notes that the king of Heaven returns part of it as a gift to the man or woman of prayer. This is the experience of 'sweetness and comfort' which presumably can be likened to joy: our good works give joy to others, and something of that is also given to us. However even this is a gift, a grace, and cannot always be presumed; nor can good works be done simply in order to gain some sense of satisfaction from them.

What is stressed is that the tree must bear fruit, and this fruit is nothing other than 'good works'. Here the image of the marriage and the image of the tree converge: both must bear the fruit of good works. So this call to love, which is the essence of contemplative prayer, is not a gift we can indulge for its own sake. The gift is given in order to bear fruit. This, of course, is the clear teaching of scripture. Indeed the image of the tree is one much favoured by the Lord himself:

> So, every sound tree bears good fruit, but the bad tree bears evil fruit. A sound tree cannot bear evil fruit, nor can a bad tree bear good fruit. Every tree that does not bear good fruit is cut down and thrown into the fire. Thus you will know them by their fruits *(Mt 7:17-20)*.

The image is quite clear. The tree has no value unless it bears good fruit. And in John's gospel we have a similar idea in the case of the vine (Jn 15:1-11). Here the close connection between the vine and the branches is used to express the idea at the heart of our author's teaching. In contemplative prayer the human being is called to a close intimacy with God. The life of God courses through the hearts of those who respond to his call, just as the sap flows from vine to branches. The same principle of life is at work in both. And a severe pruning, something of a death, is required in order to enable new life to burgeon.

We can be very confident that the call to contemplation is not a quest for some form of religious experience. The gospel imperative is clear enough and repeated in various ways:

> Not every one who says to me, 'Lord, Lord,' shall enter the kingdom of heaven, but he who does the will of my father who is in heaven *(Mt 7:21)*.

It might prove emotionally or aesthetically satisfying to call on the Lord. But the Lord asks us to *do* what he asks (Lk 6:46) and not merely to voice pleasing sentiments. It is those who hear the word of God and keep it, who have an intimate relationship with Christ (Lk 8:21). Indeed those who hear the word of God and keep it are 'blessed' (Lk 11:27). In contemplative prayer we are, as we have seen, steeped in the word of God reduced to its essential elements (see chapter 12) and so the contemplative is literally saturated with God. St Teresa expressed it thus in one of her typically clear images:

> ... the soul has a capacity for great fruition ... as water permeates and is drunk in by a sponge, so it seemed to me, did the Divinity fill my soul, which in a certain sense had the fruition and possession of the Three Persons *(Relations III 9)*.

So the test of the genuine nature of this experience is not the outpouring of pious emotions or edifying words, being able to say 'Lord, Lord'. The only valid test is whether we have taken the word of God to our hearts and left ourselves open to its reforming influence; and this will result in 'good works'. Thus the real 'fruit' of contemplation is nothing less than love:

> The perfection of the human being is nothing else but a unity between God and the human being in perfect love. This perfection is so high and so pure in itself; above human understanding, that it can be neither known or perceived in itself. But where the properties that pertain to this perfection are truly seen and perceived, it is likely that the reality itself is there ... (These properties) are the virtues. Now if you will truly look at this work in the soul and the nature and condition of each virtue separately, you will find that all the virtues are clearly and perfectly comprehended in it, without any deviation or corruption of purpose.
>
> Here I do not intend to discuss any virtue in particular. It is not necessary to do so for they are touched on in some manner in various other places in my own writing. For this work, if it be truly understood, is that reverent affection and 'the fruit separated from the tree' of which I spoke in my little *Epistle of Prayer (Privy Counsel 7)*.

In this moving passage we are reminded that our human growth is intimately linked to, and indeed inseparable from, the divine life within us. The God who creates, redeems and calls in love is all the while making us the kind of men and women he wishes us to be. Here we find harmonised the individual and corporate aspects of life which we discussed in the first chapter. The human being is the recipient of mystery: the mystery of God's presence. This is nothing other than the gift of Baptism. But Baptism is not merely a gift given; like any form of life it must either grow or stagnate; it must flourish or be stifled. The man who hid the talent he had been given was condemned for failing to let it grow and flourish (Mt 25:24-30).

So the mystery within us must be enabled to grow; we must be increasingly at home with the 'cloud of unknowing' under whose shadow we walk; we must have an ever deepening realisation that we are the Ark where the Lord dwells, the temple of the Holy Spirit (1 Cor 6:19). All these concepts are at the centre of human growth. No one of us lives for self alone; 'no man is an island' as John Donne reminded us.

So our author tells us that the fruit must be separated from the tree. The 'fruit' of baptism is the presence of God; 'godliness'. And that must be separated from the tree. That is, we must offer godliness to others as a gift and a grace. The gift is not a gift just for self, the gift is given that it might be shared.

> The work shall witness to what the experience works *(Privy Counsel 7)*.

What the grace of contemplation is working within us will be witnessed by our manner of living, our 'life-style'; that is by the exercise of the virtues. In sum, the virtues will amount to nothing less than a humanity which is as it should be: an image of God developing more and more into a likeness of God. The 'cloud of unknowing', the mystery of God within us, will manifest itself:

> As Solomon says, 'it shall be life to your soul' within you by your tender love for God 'and grace to your countenance' in the truth of your teaching, the seemly manner in which you control your physical bearing and your way of living among your fellow Christians *(Privy Counsel 5)*.

In this section of the *Privy Counsel* our author is giving an analysis of the book of Proverbs (Prov 3:3-14 and 21-26). The 'cloud of unknowing' is the real wisdom which makes for true human blessedness. It is more precious than silver or gold. If we keep it, and heed it, it will surely colour our whole manner of living:

> keep sound wisdom and discretion;
> let them not escape from your sight,
> and they will be life for your soul
> and adornment for your neck.
> Then you will walk on your way securely
> and your foot will not stumble.
> If you sit down you will not be afraid;
> when you lie down your sleep will be sweet.
> Do not be afraid of sudden panic,
> or of the ruin of the wicked when it comes;
> for the Lord will be your confidence
> and will keep your foot from being caught
> *(Prov 3:21-26).*

The person who walks the way of this 'wisdom' is one who has the mysterious presence of God within, and so is adorned with all the virtues:

> For virtue is nothing else but an ordinary and measured affection, plainly directed unto God for his own sake *(The Cloud 12).*

Thus virtue is not so much a catalogue of things to be avoided and things to be done. Virtue is simply the love of God in the soul of the Christian who thereby avoids evil and does good. As our author sums it up so succinctly:

> Prayer in itself is, strictly speaking, nothing else but a devout intention directed towards God for the getting of good things and the removing of evils *(The Cloud 39).*

Thus when we see a good human being we do not merely witness a collection of good qualities or a succession of fine actions. When we see such a human performance we also 'see' God in some sense. Thus St Irenaeus in his celebrated work *Against Heresies* argues that through the prophets and especially in the humanity of Christ, we 'see' God; so all Christians, who are alive to the grace of their baptism, show forth God: 'the glory of God is a living man' (*Against Heresies IV, 20. 7*). As our author has so often repeated, we know God through his actions: he creates, redeems and calls in love. What he is in himself is shrouded in mystery. Similarly with human beings. We can know other humans by their 'fruits', by their deeds, but we do not know the mystery of the other human being. The philosopher K. Jaspers, points to this mystery when he reminds us:

> Man, in his empirical reality, can be a subject of research in many directions; but man is always more than he knows or can know about himself
> *(quoted in* W Kaufmann, *Existentialism p 151).*

Yet the same author goes on to say that 'Man is less certain of himself than ever'. Is there a crisis of humanity? Gabriel Marcel, the French Catholic philosopher is among those who would claim that there is. He argues that we live in an age of rampant self assertiveness and acquisitiveness. Are people largely seeking 'self-interests'? He writes:

> A crazy idea has taken possession of an increasing number of misguided individuals (that) to serve has something humiliating about it for him who serves ... those among the leaders or rulers who have allowed the sense of their responsibility to waste away in the depth of their being, have helped to an extent it is impossible to exaggerate to prepare the way for this crisis in the idea of service ... the general lowering of the human tone, above all of course since 1918, probably constitutes the most outstanding fact of our recent history, and one perhaps which best explains our disaster
> *(Homo Viator 127).*

While Marcel was speaking of the defeat of France in the Second World War, his comments might still have some relevance. While we should not romanticise the pre-1914 period, we still must admit to living in an age in which we witness great technological advances going hand in hand with an aggressive self-assertiveness; the quest for larger and still larger profits; and the ready resort to violence as a solution for difficulties. Perhaps the media feed us an unbalanced diet which largely overlooks the heroic and the selfless in the human story; but still the media view is the way many people perceive our contemporary world. However we may assess it we cannot doubt that the mystic has a mission in our day. If by mystic we mean one who has some sensitivity to the existence of the deep mystery in human nature, then there is certainly a mission to 'save'. And this not simply to save something so nebulous as 'humanity', but rather to save human beings. While not denying the place for all manner of 'development' the late Pope Paul VI saw the basic need as one for the development of human beings:

> If development calls for an ever-growing number of technical experts, even more necessary still is the deep thought and reflection of wise men in search of a new 'humanism', one which will enable our contemporaries to enjoy the higher values of love and friendship, of prayer and contemplation, and thus *find themselves* (italics added). This is what will guarantee our authentic development — the transition from less than human conditions to truly human ones *(Populorum Progressio)*.

Human beings can only 'find themselves' and grow if there are a number of conditions. But surely one is the quality of humanity, and that must be a basic one. Our world needs people who have a genuine sense of serving rather than exploiting; who will respect and love the mystery in others, rather than be seeking for status and things for self. It is here that the contemplative has a role. We are often impressed with the power of evil: our news reports are saturated with bombings, robbings, starvation, the drug traffic and the rest. But we also need to realise the power to save exercised by good human beings. In a very charming story in Genesis Abraham asks the Lord to spare Sodom if there were but 50 righteous people within the city; but then he asked that the city be spared for 45, and eventually reduced his plea to 10 (Gen 18:22-33). It is an interesting case of a wily Semite arguing for a better deal; it is also a good example of the believer's familiarity with the Lord; but it is also a reminder that even a handful of good people can be a saving leaven in a society.

17. Christian Maturity

> *Virtue is nothing other than an ordered and controlled affection which has God himself alone as its single object. For God himself is the pure cause of all virtue: so that if you can be stirred to any one virtue by some other cause, even though God be partly the motive (or indeed the chief motive) the virtue is said to be 'imperfect'. This can be seen in one or two virtues, rather than by looking at all of them. Humility and charity are two good examples, for if you have these two, you need no others: you have all* (The Cloud 12).

Our growth into Christian maturity is not a simple matter; we must be weaned from 'lesser' motives for doing good so that our actions take on a God-oriented quality. We need to recognise that our actions can have a strange mixture about them: we can surprise ourselves when we ponder our real motives for doing what might seem generous and noble deeds. We are 'scattered' and divided and in need of an inner healing and unity. It is a sign of our growing maturity when we can act on motives that are good, simple and consistent. Sometimes our actions appear better than they really are; at other times we are motivated by high ideals one moment only to find that they soon evaporate; or we might have genuinely Christian aspirations which we cannot adequately translate into words and deeds.

Christian maturity means that we act on good principles in a reliable and predictable manner. In contemplative prayer, we turn our longing to the only One who can give us an inner unity and who can facilitate a developing harmony between heart and deed. And such a growth towards inner unity and reliability involves a process of cleansing and healing. The crooked ways of our inconsistencies need to be made straight, and the valleys of our lesser motives filled with a grace that enables us to walk on a higher plain. It is only God who can so unify and heal us that we act with a simplicity and wholeness; contemplative prayer involves a real growth in our humanity.

As we look at this growth in 'virtue' our author is very clear about the significance of two virtues: humility and charity. These are, in fact, the foundation and the completion of our human growth as Christians. In seeing the essential role of these two virtues our author finds an echo in Walter Hilton:

> How can any sinner alive . . . take any pleasure or feel any confidence in himself on account of anything he can achieve through his bodily powers or natural reason? For nothing is of any value without love and charity towards his fellow-Christians, and this charity cannot be acquired by any personal efforts. It is the free gift of God granted to humble souls . . . *(Ladder of Perfection I, 68).*

The text favoured by many classical spiritual writers is:

> God resists the proud
> but gives grace to the humble
> *(Jas 4:6).*

This humility has been variously described by classical writers: our author opts for a basic realism as his understanding of the term:

> Humility is nothing other than a true knowledge and feeling of yourself as you are. For surely if you truly see and feel yourself as you are, you should be truly humble. There are two causes of this humility. One is the filth,

wretchedness and frailty of humanity which has come about because of sin. It is always valuable to feel something of this so long as you are alive, no matter how holy you are. The other cause of humility is the inexhaustible love of God in himself: before him all nature quakes, all scholars are fools and all saints and angels are blind *(The Cloud 13).*

So humility is simply the truth about ourselves; and a mature person is one with a very perceptive understanding of self. The word itself relates to the Latin word 'humus', meaning 'earth'. Humility has a 'feet-on-the-ground' aspect to it: it places us fairly and squarely in the real world. One part of this truth about self is that each of us is part of a larger world; we inhabit an environment. We are members of a world that has been badly damaged or flawed by what we call sin. Indeed we have been touched by this from our beginning:

> Behold I was brought forth in iniquity,
> And in sin did my mother conceive me
> *(Ps 51 (50):5).*

Yet this world of people, things and events is not totally flawed: it still sends forth brilliant signals which tell of the beauty and love of God:

> (God) did not leave himself without witness, for he did good and gave you from heaven rains and fruitful seasons, satisfying your hearts with food and gladness *(Acts 14:17).*

The Christian must take a stand in the midst of this ambivalent world, deriving blessings from it and contributing to it. Yet with an inner freedom which refuses to be enslaved to its beauty or defeated by its darker side. The Christian steeped in prayer knows that it would profit nothing to gain mastery over all these surroundings, and suffer the loss of one's soul (Mt 16:26). It is a sign of great human maturity when we can get both this world and ourselves in proper focus.

In recent years a great Christian, Dietrich Bonhoeffer, writing from prison told his parents:

> I have in front of me the gay bunch of dahlias that you brought me yesterday; it reminds me of the lovely hour that I was able to have with you, and of the garden, and in general of how beautiful the world can be in these autumn days. One of Storm's verses that I came across the other day just about expresses this mood, and keeps going through my head like a tune that one cannot get rid of:
>
> And however crazy,
> Or Christian, or unchristian things may be outside,
> This world, this beautiful world
> Is quite indestructible.
>
> All that it needed to bring that home to one is a few gay autumn flowers, the view from the cell window, and half an hour's 'exercise' in the prison yard, where there are, in fact, a few beautiful chestnut and lime trees *(Letters and Papers from Prison [Letter of 13 October 1943]).*

What a strange, mixed-up world: the confines of a prison, the cruelty of his Nazi oppressors, the beauty of flowers, the love of dear ones! And in the midst of it all Bonhoeffer took his stand with quiet realism.

As we seek to discover this realism we can look, not merely at ourselves in our environment, but also at self in 'isolation' as it were. Here, our author is sure that we have been showered with many blessings: we have been made in the image and likeness of God *(The Cloud 13)*; we are the spiritual temples of God *(The Cloud 71)* and we have been 'onyd to God in spirit' *(The Cloud 67)*; and as such we are called to perfection:

148 • The Cloud

> Our Lord Jesus Christ calls us himself in the gospel; where he tells us that we should be perfect by grace as he himself is by nature *(The Cloud 15)*.

It is also clear that he held a very exalted notion of humanity before the sin of Adam. Indeed he seems to interpret the 'fall' as a rejection of the grace of contemplative prayer:

> For all sickness and corruption took root in the flesh when the soul turned from this exercise *(Privy Counsel 5)*.

So a 'reformation' of humanity involves the renewal of this grace; we cannot be truly human without it:

> If you had been reformed by grace to the state of original innocence (enjoyed by Adam) you would always have the help of grace to be in command of the strivings of the heart *(The Cloud 4)*.

All this implies that in our present human state we have lost an inner unity and a sense of purpose; we have lost command of our hearts and so are 'scattered' over numerous transient aims that amount to a state of 'sickness and corruption'. So in this virtue of humility we take a realistic look at this damaged self. We see that, like the world about us, we have an ambivalence: we are graced in so many ways yet we carry the burden of sin. But when we come to know self, does this mean a detailed self-analysis? Not at all. As we have seen, our author wants his disciple to be faithful to the practice of reconciliation; but he does not want continued self analysis. Nor indeed would he want us to seek the truth about ourselves simply from psychological testing of various kinds, however much they might help at times. As we have seen, he expressly warns against too introspective a stance (see chapter 6).

Nor, on the other hand does humility mean that we feel inadequate and inferior and creep into a corner in an attitude of self depreciation. Such a stance is more akin to the pride it supposedly rejects; and it often closely resembles sheer laziness ... But a knowledge of self that is prompted simply by a consideration of self is 'imperfect'. So while it is wise to take a realistic look at ourselves, we do well to remember our author's teaching that this is only 'imperfect' humility, or self knowledge. Many people find it all too tempting to linger here, to subject themselves to critical scrutiny, and become overly anxious about their performance as human beings and Christians. It is all too easy to be drawn into a vortex of self-pity and useless regrets. Such attitudes can prove crippling and possibly destructive. We must move on something deeper as the basis of our self knowledge. We must turn our gaze from self to God:

> And therefore by toil and sweat in every way you can and may, seek to obtain a true knowledge and feeling of yourself as you are. And I believe that soon after that you will have a true knowledge and feeling of God as he is *(The Cloud 12)*.

We have already seen this remarkable passage (chapter 6). Our growth is to be one that takes us away from self to a knowledge of God. We recognise the blessings we have, and we realise that they come from God; we face our sinfulness, the 'lump' of sin which we carry, and we realise that we must throw ourselves upon the mercy of God. We need God: that is the truth about ourselves. A true recognition of 'self' then leads us to an awareness of God. Such a teaching implies that as we look at self in 'isolation' we also put the self back into its true environment. To have 'self-knowledge' in this sense is urged by all the great spiritual writers. St Catherine of Siena links these two fundamental virtues together:

> No virtue can have life in it except from charity, and charity is nurtured and mothered by humility. You will find humility in the knowledge of yourself when you see that even your existence comes not from yourself but from me, for I loved you before you came into being. And in my unspeakable love for you I willed to create you anew in grace. So I washed you and made you a new creation in the blood that my only begotten Son poured out with such burning love.
>
> This blood gives you knowledge of the truth when knowledge of yourself leads you to shed the cloud of selfish love *(The Dialogue 4)*.

Walter Hilton adopts a very similar attitude, and also speaks of 'perfect' humility as that which has God alone as its motive:

> A soul comes to perfect humility through the contemplation and knowledge of God. For when the Holy Spirit illumines the soul's understanding ... how God is All in all and does all, the soul feels such love and joy at this experience that it forgets itself and devotes itself entirely to the contemplation of God ... As a result of this vision of God it feels and sees itself as it is, so that it gives up considering and relying on itself, and devotes itself wholly to the contemplation of God *(Ladder of Perfection II, 37)*.

Implicit in all such teaching is the thought that we should not take ourselves too seriously! It is, indeed, a very good thing if we can occasionally laugh at ourselves; we can be very foolish when we adopt various guises that would inflate our worth and importance. In a letter advising that we laugh at ourselves, Abbot Chapman goes on to say that it is a good thing if we have 'dissatisfaction with ourselves — provided we also have confidence in God' *(Spiritual Letters p 153)*. And this is always the point to which 'perfect' humility, that is perfect self-knowledge must return. Hence our author gives sound practical advice. Have a general, realistic view of self:

> Mean by sin a 'lump', you know not what in detail, just simply yourself. I think that this blind beholding of sin, congealed into a lump, is nothing other than yourself *(The Cloud 37).*

And in a practical, matter-of-fact way, we place this sinful self into the hands of God. In the opening pages of *Privy Counsel* he advises such a realistic acceptance of self; aware of our basic poverty we *do* the practical and sensible thing about it: we place ourselves in the hands of God:

> 'What I am Lord, I offer to you, for it is truly yourself (to whom I surrender)'. And keep in mind simply, plainly and frankly that you are as you are, and this can be done without any form of curiosity *(Privy Counsel 1).*

Here we accept the truth; and this enables us to grow to our maturity as Christians. Once we are 'in God' we have the only One who can give us an inner unity, purpose and consistency. We need to remember that this is not merely some form of intellectual attitude we reason ourselves into: it is essentially something we must *do*, despite what our thoughts and feelings might be dictating. In our prayer we take the attitude of being simply there, before God, as this 'lump' of sin. In such an attitude we take the advice of Peter:

> Humble yourselves therefore under the mighty hand of God, that in due time he may exalt you. Cast all your anxieties on him, for he cares about you *(2 Pt 5:6-7).*

In speaking of this growth our author illustrates his teaching by using the Mary and Martha story. It is a significant aspect of his very encouraging attitude that he does not begin this story with the Mary-Martha incident; he begins with the conversion of Mary the sinner. Mary is a sign of hope that a sinner can be called to contemplative prayer. Mary's attitude was one of genuine humility: her knowledge of self was not simply some form of introspection. Her awareness of self was caused by her awareness of God:

> When our Lord said to Mary, the typical representative of all sinners who are called to the contemplative life: 'Your sins are forgiven you', it was not because of her great sorrow, nor the remembrance of her sins, nor even the meekness she had when she considered her own wretchedness. Why then? Surely because she loved much *(The Cloud 16)*.

When we turn our gaze from self to God we place ourselves where we truly belong; as sinners we simply stand not merely *before* but *in* this God in whom we live, move and have our being. (Acts 17:28) We are in our true atmosphere; we are like the fish thrown back into the water.

A simple story in the collection of 'sayings' of the Desert Fathers gives a clue as to how all these factors come together to facilitate our growth as Christians.

> An old man was asked, 'What is humility?' He replied, 'It is when your brother sins against you and you forgive him before he comes to ask for forgiveness' *(The Wisdom of the Desert Fathers [ed Benedicta Ward] no 172)*.

Jesus Christ 'emptied' himself and became a servant; he is the one who takes on our condition and so is 'humble', of this earth; in him humility and love come together; just as he is truly love itself, so he is also 'humility itself'; by our baptism we are immersed in the forgiveness which he brings us; it is this which enables us to grow. He makes us free.

18. Freedom

> *A simple, spontaneous thought ... which comes to your will and your understanding, is not a sin imputed to you. It is, however, the effect of original sin from which you were cleansed in your baptism but which still lessens your control over your faculties* (The Cloud 10).

Here our author adverts to the ambivalent situation of the Christian. We can be plagued by all manner of spontaneous thoughts and feelings but if they are not owned by us, they are not sinful. In our baptism we were given the freedom of God's children, yet there still lurks within us an instinctive attraction to evil. We have been given the gift of God's grace but we still have to grow into its fulness. We are in the kingdom of God and truly its citizens, but an enemy still prowls the forest. We have been given the gift of life, but also have frightening capabilities of self destruction. Walter Hilton clearly articulates the ambivalence of our situation. He distinguishes between reformation in faith and reformation in faith and experience:

> (Reformation in faith) may be had while the image of sin is still active within us; for though a person may be conscious of nothing but sinful impulses and carnal desires, yet if he does not willingly assent to them, he may be reformed by faith to the likeness of God. But the second type of reformation eradicates from the soul all carnal impulses and worldly desires, and allows no imperfections to survive
> *(Ladder of Perfection II, 5).*

The first reformation, that of faith, is effected by the sacraments. But sacramental grace does not destroy the need for human effort and lived experience: rather, the sacraments enable us to grow through time, experience and struggle. An essential part of this growth is prayer:

> So, if you are determined to stand and not fall, never give up your firm intention; but constantly beat away at that cloud of unknowing that is between you and your God, with the sharp dart of longing love. Loath to think of anything less than God, and do not desist from your purpose for anything that might arise. For this alone, by itself, destroys the root and ground of sin. No matter how much you might fast, keep vigil, rise early, sleep on boards, wear uncomfortable clothing — yes, even if it were lawful (and it is not!), pluck out your eyes, cut out your tongue, amputate your private parts and inflict on your body all the pain that you can or may think: all this would do nothing for you. The urge and the impulse to sin would still be with you *(The Cloud 12)*.

This is the consistent teaching of our author. Bodily mortifications are merely a means to an end and must be practised with moderation and discretion. Such dramatic deeds are not, in themselves, sufficient to ensure the radical healing of the human being, they are not an assured way to God. They are only of value in so far as they are expressions of a deep personal love for God, and of our desire to be liberated from selfishness.

> Let be then, all such things as these — silence and speaking, fasting and eating, solitude or company. Take no notice of them. You do not know what they mean and I beg you not to seek to understand them ... For if you are eager to achieve your spiritual purpose, you have a sufficient method and means: you do not need any more than the actual thought of God, with a reverent stirring of abiding love. The only means you have of reaching God is God himself. However you must keep whole this stirring

of love, that you may experience grace in your heart, and not let your spiritual aim be scattered *(Stirrings)*.

Keeping one's mind and heart fixed on the 'unknown' is in itself a 'discipline', and a real Christian asceticism. Within the framework of that experience we have the means we need to grow in our Christian life. Not for him any of the histrionics of contemporary movements such as the Flagellants who experienced renewed popularity in many parts of Europe after the Black Death. The important point that the author makes in these passages is that something dramatic is being done to us during contemplative prayer. The God we know as creator, redeemer and lover is slowly renewing the human being who lovingly leaves him or herself at his disposal. God is the only means we have of reaching God.

Even when we are most fragile and vulnerable it is God himself and not any penitential practices that must come to our aid. We can be plagued by all manner of thoughts and feelings that could prove destructive, and our author advises us that we must seek escape in the mystery of God:

> Try to look, as it were, over your shoulder, seeking something else — namely God enclosed in the cloud of unknowing *(The Cloud 32)*.

But even this might not prove useful in moments of great anxiety and temptation. So he suggests another approach which brings us back to that reality which we call humility:

> When you feel that you can in no wise put down these thoughts, cower down under them as a poor wretch and a coward overcome in battle, and think that it is mere folly to strive any longer against them. And thus you yield yourself to God while you are in the hands of your enemies. You feel as though you were overcome for ever. I beg you to pay careful heed to this advice, for it seems to me that when you put it to the test, it will dissolve all

> opposition. If this device is truly understood it is nothing other than a true knowledge and feeling of yourself as you are: wretched, filthy and worse than nothing. This indeed is humility. And this humility deserves to have God himself come down, in his might, and avenge you of your enemies, and take you up and cherish you ... as a father does for a child *(The Cloud 32)*.

There can be little doubt that this device is a real self-discipline, the acceptance of a cross. It is a real turning away from self and towards God. Here too, we accept self as we really are: often hopelessly fragile and under the spell of evil. And we throw that weak, tempted and broken self into the arms of Mercy. Indeed whenever we come to prayer, we come as sinners, as people in need of ever deeper conversion and healing. So our author is consistently clear about the healing power of contemplation. As we stand before God, simply wanting him, we appear to be doing less and less. But he is all the while active as the God who is creating, healing and loving. The quiet, undramatic moments of prayer are saturated with an activity that is beyond our ken: we are in the womb of God. This is the quiet hidden world where the seed of grace, which is the Word heard and Sacrament received, is enabled to come to full fruition.

As we have seen (chapter 3) our author sees this as the living and healing touch of God:

> Take the good gracious God just as he is, and simply lay him on your sick self just as you are ... Touching him is an endless help as we see from the evidence of the Gospel: 'If I touch even his garments, I shall be made well' *(Privy Counsel 2)*.

But we must not reduce this healing process to a bland, nebulous experience. This is no numbing anaesthetic. As we are told in the book of Job, the God who heals, does so in a way that involves some pain and suffering:

> He wounds, but he binds up;
> he smites, but his hands heal
> *(Job 5:18).*

This process of being healed of the 'root and ground of sin' involves that radical transformation of self which is a 'dark night'. In his own graphic words our author explains something of the pain involved:

> Your affection is wonderfully changed in the spiritual experience of the 'nothing' when it is achieved 'nowhere'. For the first time that you look at it, you will find all the particular sins (whether in thought or deed) that you have committed since you were born, secretly and darkly depicted on it. And no matter how you turn about, they will appear before your eyes; until such time that after much hard work, many sore sighs, and copious bitter tears, you have in great part rubbed them away
> *(The Cloud 69).*

The overpowering presence of God makes us aware of our sinfulness; our evil deeds become all the more stark. Like someone who turns up at a dinner dressed in gardening clothes when everyone else is in formal attire. The situation is enough to make the sensitive person feel totally incongruous and out of place. As we face this fact of our sinfulness we are tempted to despair and turn aside from the contemplative quest:

> Sometimes in this struggle you think that you are looking at hell; for you feel some despair of reaching perfection and spiritual peace out of all this suffering. Many people come thus far on the inward journey but because of the intense pain they experience and the lack of consolation, they go back to the consideration of bodily things. They seek the external comforts of the flesh, in place of the spiritual consolation which they have not yet deserved, but which they would have deserved had they persevered
> *(The Cloud 69).*

There certainly come times when we feel the effort is too great and the gains too meagre. At such moments *the* asceticism is simply persevering; and such persevering means not merely persevering in prayer but also in the simple round of life's tasks. St Teresa expressed it thus:

> Everything depends on your having a great and most resolute determination never to halt until you reach your journey's end no matter what may happen, whatever the consequences, cost what it will . . . *(Way of Perfection 21).*

This is a teaching which she also expresses with great emphasis in the *Interior Castle II*. And Walter Hilton, so close to our author in many of his teachings sees this as the crucial period in a person's growth: it explains why so comparatively few are 'reformed by faith and experience'. People fail to make a 'whole hearted effort' at this stage *(Ladder of Perfection II, 18)*. For his part, our author holds out the hope that this painful and crucial stage will not be without some tangible encouragement:

> For if you persevere you will, at some time, feel some comfort and have some hope of perfection, for you begin to feel and indeed see, that many of your former particular sins are in great part rubbed away by the help of grace. Nevertheless even in the midst of such pain there is some consolation, for you know it will come to an end for it waxes less and less. And so you will begin to call it purgatory rather than hell. Sometimes you see no particular sin written thereon, but you still think of sin as a lump; nothing other than yourself. And then it can be called the ground and pain of original sin. Sometimes you think it is paradise or heaven because of the wonderful and sweet comforts and joys and blessed virtues that you discover. Sometimes you think it is God because of the rest and peace you experience.
>
> Yet, think what you like, you will always find that there is a cloud of unknowing between you and your God *(The Cloud 69).*

So there are moments when we are tempted to stop making the effort. There could be no clearer indication that our author is not tinged with something akin to 'quietism'. Never does he let us think that the mystery of God's grace implies a cessation of human effort and a sharing in the cross of Christ. When things seem at their darkest and least hopeful, there is a need to persevere in the midst of what is a cloud; perhaps a cloud of despair and a cloud of weakness. But it is in fact, still the cloud of forgetting in which we are being painfully stripped of self. This cloud of forgetting and the cloud of unknowing are the two things of which we can be certain. Whatever pleasing or painful feelings we might experience from time to time, we need to be brought back to these basic realities.

There does come a time when we are tempted to seek distraction in other things: to pander to our sense of pleasure; to cushion our lives with trivial comforts; to seek the ease of our own particular Egypt rather than face the harsh realities of the pilgrimage; to find refuge in the world of noise and movement. But it is obvious that if we persevere in the pilgrimage, guided by the 'cloud', we shall grow. We are being slowly 'converted', turned from self to God. 'Forgetting' our sinful selves is nothing other than letting go our grasp of the things that pander to self and so result in sin. Ever so slowly our centre of gravity is changing; the pain of selfishness remains but there is also a pull in another direction. The 'leash of longing' of which the author spoke is gently drawing us towards the mystery of God. Consciousness of particular sins gives way to a general sense of sinfulness, that 'lump' of sin which is self.

But whatever the consolations might be they are *not* God. The 'cloud of unknowing' remains. So we are slowly being taught that we are not seeking a feeling of spiritual well-being: that is only selfishness under the guise of piety. We are seeking God himself. So we are not merely being liberated from sin; we are also being liberated from our own spiritual experience and from the thraldom of our own 'religion'. We will not be too distressed whether our Eucharist comes in all the glory of a plainchant Mass in a medieval cathedral, or is accompanied by a joyous Mozart Mass in a flamboyant baroque church, or whether it is celebrated in the simple and homely style of the post-Vatican II liturgy. Each of these has an abiding and timely value: but in the end we shall be satisfied with the Word of Life and the Bread of Heaven. And similarly in our private prayer, we will not be too concerned to seek 'religious experience': we shall be privileged enough to stand before the cloud of unknowing. We shall have lost a life and found our life in God.

This deep inner freedom must be won through the strange combination of grace and human endeavour. For our part we cannot remain indecisive: either we choose to follow the hard path of freedom, or we sink ever deeper into the servitude of sin

> By this exercise you are to be restored again. Neglect of this work results in your falling deeper and deeper into sin and further and further from God. And by perseverance and continual working in this exercise alone, you become more and more free from sin and nearer to God *(The Cloud 4)*.

But in a very balanced way our author does not see this as merely a 'spiritual' work and therefore good; and set over against what is material and evil. The whole human being must be restored to wholeness, health and freedom.

> For as Solomon says: 'It is health to all weakness and ills of the flesh'. And rightly so for all sickness and corruption befell the flesh when the soul turned from this work. So all health will come to the flesh when the soul, through the grace of Jesus, the chief worker, returns again to this work. You can only have this through the mercy of Jesus and your loving consent *(Privy Counsel 5)*.

The author's teaching makes good sense. The sort of company we keep has an effect on our whole personalities. This commonplace wisdom is echoed in the scriptures:

> Iron whets iron,
> friend shapes friend
> *(Prov 27:17 [Knox]).*

So the constant contact with God in the depths of one's being has its results. These are summed up in the oft repeated teaching:

> In this work the soul dries up the root and ground of sin which remain there, even after your confession; however busy you might be with holy things *(The Cloud 28).*

So we are gradually being set free from what Hilton calls 'the root of all sins . . . a false and misplaced love of self' (*Ladder of Perfection I, 42*). Among other things this freedom manifests itself in a marked indifference to the opinions of others. Mary was indifferent to the remarks made by her sister; so we too will be free from undue concern over what others might think (*The Cloud 23*). J H Newman portrayed this freedom in a character in a novel:

> Charles's characteristic, perhaps above anything else, was an habitual sense of the Divine Presence; a sense which, of course, did not ensure uninterrupted conformity of thought and deed to itself, but still, there it was — the pillar of the cloud before him and guiding him. He felt himself to be God's creature, and responsible to Him — God's possession, not his own. He had a great wish to succeed in the schools; a thrill came over him when he thought of it; but ambition was not his life; he could have reconciled himself in a few minutes to failure
> *(Loss and Gain pp 220-1).*

This deep inner freedom also extends to things as well as to the opinions of others. Indeed our author is very clear about the deepening freedom from possessiveness:

> You can firmly trust, whoever you are that has truly turned from the world to God, that he will send you one of two things, without any attention to it on your part: either an abundance of what is necessary, or the strength in body and patience in spirit, to endure want. What does it matter then which of these you have? It is all the same to the true contemplative *(The Cloud 23)*.

This points to a liberation from possessiveness and acquisitiveness, two of the besetting cancers of contemporary western society. The person who practises this form of prayer has a mind and heart set on God, not on the gifts of God. This is the true freedom spoken of in the gospel:

> Do not lay up for yourselves treasures on earth, where moth and rust consume and where thieves break in and steal, but lay up for yourselves treasures in heaven ... For where your treasure is, there will be your heart also *(Mt 6:19-21)*.

But as the contemplative gains an ever greater liberation from acquisitiveness and materialism, so he or she does not become detached from the world and aloof from its sufferings. The author spoke of our freedom from things *(The Cloud 23*, above) just before he made his most profound remarks concerning love for others. In our day the contemplative should have a deep sensitivity to the suffering of others; and also when called to do so, to speak with a prophetic voice of the injustices done to others. In his encyclical letter On Social Concerns (*Sollicitudo Rei Socialis*, 1988), Pope John Paul II lamented the contemporary materialism which 'makes people slaves of *possessions* and of immediate gratification (in which) the more one possesses the more one wants' (no 28). The Pope invited all Christians to seek to alleviate injustices:

> We can find here a new invitation to bear witness together to our common convictions concerning the dignity of humans created by God, redeemed by Christ, made holy by the Spirit and called upon in this world to live a life in conformity with this dignity *(Sollicitudo Rei Socialis 47)*.

These words echo our author's teaching concerning God being Creator, Redeemer and Lover. The one steeped in the experience of such a God, should have a true and abiding sensitivity to the dignity of others: the contemplative should be free to serve.

19. Love

Charity is nothing other than the love of God for himself above all creatures; and the love of other people for God's sake, just as you love yourself. It is quite clear that in contemplation God is loved for himself above all creatures. For, as has already been said, this work is simply a naked intention reaching out to God for his own sake. I call it a 'naked intention' because in this matter a perfect apprentice does not ask to be spared pain, or to be generously rewarded. Nothing is sought but God himself. This is so much the case that the contemplative is indifferent to pain or joy, so long as the will of the loved one is fulfilled. So it is clear that in contemplation God is perfectly loved for himself; and above all creatures. For in this prayer the perfect worker will not permit the remembrance of the holiest creature that God ever made to have any share.

Experience proves that in this very work the second and lower branch of love, that is love for your fellow Christians, is truly and perfectly fulfilled. For the very reason that in this work the perfect worker has no special regard for any individual, whether such be kinsman or stranger, friend or foe. The contemplative regards all people alike as friends and none as foes. So much so that all who cause you pain and do you mischief in this life, are considered your real and special friends and you are moved to wish them as much good as you would wish the dearest friend you have (The Cloud 24).

This is a passage which gives us the 'essential' *Cloud*. Nowhere else does the author so succinctly sum up the whole of his teaching on the nature of this prayer and its effects on the lives of its practitioners. He simply reiterates the first and greatest of the commandments:

> Hear, O Israel: the Lord our God is one Lord: and you shall love the Lord your God with all your heart ... soul ... (and) ... might *(Deut 6:4-5)*.

And as it is repeated in the gospel:

> You shall Love the Lord your God with all your heart ... soul ... strength ... (and) mind *(Lk 10:27)*.

In contemplative prayer there is a 'naked intention' reaching out to God: it is a desire that is willing to be stripped of all else. So strong is this desire that it asks neither to be spared the pains of life, nor to be generously rewarded for what is done. This desire means simply wanting God; it does not count the cost or calculate the benefits. Julian of Norwich expressed the same view when she taught that we should be indifferent to pain or pleasure. God always holds us in his hands:

> alike in 'weal or woe' ...
> both are equally his love
> *(Revelations 15)*.

We are not concerned about the 'state' we are in, so long as that 'state' or situation is 'in God'.

In this form of prayer our intention is also 'naked' because it is not clothed in images or sounds; in fine thoughts or words; nor is it engendered by techniques or gimmicks of any kind. It is just simply the human being, oneself as one is here and now, in all one's poverty and fragility: just that self placed in the mystery of God. Although there is nothing we can think or say, let alone any emotion we should seek to arouse: there is something we can and must *do*, we must simply and starkly 'want God'. This 'naked' prayer suggests a 'desert' and an 'aridity' which often comes in the form of a dissatisfaction with self.

As John Chapman taught:

> The great danger is that people love God for His gifts, and are always on the look out for them, and think all is lost when they have a little aridity; it is hard for them to love aridity, to desire nothing so much as to be perennially dissatisfied with themselves, and full of an entirely vague and unsatisfactory longing for something unknown and unknowable *(Spiritual Letters p 125)*.

So the form of prayer taught in *The Cloud* is not some gentle, peaceful 'awareness' of God: we must take care not to romanticise contemplative prayer into being some nebulous state of quiet contentment. It takes us into a desert; it does not matter whether the experience is accompanied by joy or pain. Our emotional states can be caused by a variety of factors. In contemplative prayer the 'worker' is not seeking how to gain or avoid any emotional state: one is seeking God. And God is loved for himself 'above all creatures'. Those creatures are sometimes our ambitions, achievements, pains and sorrows. In all of this our author is merely summing up what he has said so often: we have to put a 'cloud of forgetting' between ourselves and *all* else, even 'the remembrance of the holiest creature that God ever made'. We may at times seek some special help in moments of great trial, but the ideal is this 'naked intention' which is a 'chaste' or 'pure' love. The author makes this clear:

> Love is chaste or pure when you ask God neither to release you from suffering, nor to increase your reward, nor for the sweetness of his love in this life — unless at any particular time you seek his courteous sweetness to renew your spiritual strength lest you fail on the journey. Rather

love is chaste and pure when you seek God himself and nothing else but him *(Epistle of Prayer)*.

But now he takes us further. We are not merely to love God, we are also to love others; and there is an essential connection between the two loves. In fact they are the one love. Contemplative prayer has an effect on our lives. The author's words are literally:

> And that in this work the second and the lower branch of charity unto thine evern-Christian is verily and perfectly fulfilled, it seemeth by the proof *(The Cloud 24)*.

Here he suggests two clear points. In the first place while we are engaged in this prayer we are not merely loving God, but we are also loving others. And secondly this can be seen in some 'proof', that is by experience.

So 'in this work' we are also fulfilling the divine command of love for our fellow human beings. He has already adverted to this on occasion: this prayer helps the whole of mankind in ways that are wonderful and beyond our understanding (*The Cloud 3*). But it is also clear that in this prayer something is happening to us that alters the whole quality of our lives. Our author is very clear that we cannot expect to 'feel' better as a result of this exercise; nor can we anticipate bursting with 'insights' when it is over. But we must expect that we will be more loving towards others.

This would stand to reason. When we enter this prayer we strip self of self; and this self-emptying is not a mere negation. It is an opening for God to pour his love into our hearts. Or, to put it in another way, when we practise this prayer, we simply seek the God who is Love itself. God becomes the atmosphere we inhabit, the air we breath, the ground upon which we walk. We are available to the God whom we know as Creator, Redeemer and

Lover: he is doing something to us, he is moulding us, healing us and filling us with his love. So contemplative prayer is not a negation, or a void, nor is it some static inert human condition: it is filled with the dynamism of God. It is we who seek to be still and God who is active; we come as people poor in spirit, stripped of everything, and the Kingdom is given us. In this prayer we are 'immersed' in God: when we saturate a plain white linen cloth in dye of a certain colour, the cloth will take on that colour. When we immerse ourselves in the mystery of God, we must assume some godliness; we must come from that prayer more loving and lovable.

So the love we share with others is the love that we are being given. There is but the one love; the love we have for God and the love we have for others, are not two different functions we perform: both are made possible only because of the love that has first been given to us. A familiarity with this God of love will make us more loving. It is all summed up for us by St John:

> In this is love,
> not that we loved God,
> but that he loved us,
> and sent his Son for the expiation of our sins
> *(1 Jn 4:10).*

This is the acid test of our prayer. If we do not love others then we cannot be said to 'know' God, or have experienced God. Whatever else our 'prayer' might have been it has not been an intimate relationship with God. If our prayer does not render us less selfish and more concerned about others, then it has not been prayer. If on the other hand it has been a living encounter with the God who is Love, then it will influence our dealings with others. However slowly we might be growing, we must be less selfish and more loving through our prayer.

How are we to understand this impact of God on our lives? In contemplative prayer we are being schooled in confronting the mystery of the other; we are learning not to expect easy and speedy results; we are being taught not to judge by appearances; we are left to wait patiently, rather than cajole or manipulate; we seek simply to love, that is to give without necessarily receiving tangible rewards. Contemplative prayer involves such attitudes and disciplines. But when all has been said and done we are still dealing with a mystery. We merely believe that we are in God, and that day by day, and little by little, we are being conformed to his likeness. In the end it will not be a studied programme of self-improvement: it will be the mystery of grace:

> I say that you will be made so virtuous and so loving by the power of this work that when you come away from contemplation to mix with others or to pray for your fellow Christians, you will be as much directed towards your foe as to your friend; to the stranger as much as to your kinsman. Indeed, sometimes more to foe than to friend *(The Cloud 25)*.

Here we touch the point where the Christian message reaches the heroic, and we take on something of the love of Christ for all:

> Love your enemies,
> do good to those who hate you,
> pray for those who abuse you ...
> To him who strikes you on the cheek,
> offer the other also;
> and from him who takes your cloak
> do not withold your coat as well
> *(Lk 6:26-29)*.

This love is the 'choicest fruit' which has been 'separated from the tree' which our author discussed in *Privy Counsel 8* and also *Epistle of Prayer*. Indeed this is the 'fruit' of the Spirit which St Paul describes as:

> Love, joy, peace, patience, kindness, goodness, faithfulness, gentleness, self-control ... *(Gal 5:22-23)*.

We should see these, not so much as a catalogue of blessings which we receive, as a series of blessings which we must minister to others. And the blessings are enumerated by St Paul in his description of love:

> Love is patient ... kind ... not jealous or boastful ... not arrogant or rude ... does not insist on its own way ... is not irritable or resentful ... *(1 Cor 13:4-5)*.

It has been the consistent teaching of Christian spirituality that the great test of our prayer is whether we have this love for others. In his celebrated life of St Antony (of Egypt), St Athanasius outlines the basic dynamics of prayer. Antony heard the Word of God, the call of God. One day when he entered a church he heard the gospel challenge:

> If you would be perfect go ... sell ... give ... come ... follow ... *(Mt 19:21)*.

Faced with these clear and compelling imperatives, Antony literally stripped himself of all his possessions and followed a life of great austerity: he let a 'cloud of forgetting' blanket his life. And he lived a life of prayer in the desert; he confronted the 'cloud of unknowing', the mystery of God. Commenting on the effects of this life of prayer, Athanasius made the cryptic remark:

> Thus conducting himself, Antony was beloved by all *(Life of Antony 4)*.

Prayer made Antony a more lovable human being. He was the perfect reflection of the sketch of the loving person depicted by St Paul in writing to the Corinthians. St Teresa also draws the essential link between our love for God and love for others:

> We cannot know whether we love God although there may be strong reasons for thinking so, but there can be no doubt about whether we love our neighbour or no. Be sure that in proportion as you advance in love for others, you are increasing in your love for God ... I believe that our nature is so evil that we could not feel a perfect love for our neighbour unless it were rooted in the love of God *(Interior Castle V 3)*.

The sort of love that flows from contemplation does not submerge others in emotional gush or embarrassing fuss; it does not seek to manipulate or cajole, but rather to serve. It has a measured quality and an unassuming grace without losing human warmth. Indeed our author links it with both wisdom and discernment:

> All these three — wisdom, discernment and the perfection of virtue — are all one, and well may they be called the crown of life. There are three things in a crown: firstly, gold; secondly, precious stones and thirdly the 'turrets' of the fleur-de-lis raised above the head. 'Gold' signifies wisdom; 'precious stones' discernment, and by the turrets of the fleur-de-lis I understand the perfection of virtue. Gold enriches the head, and by wisdom we govern our spiritual activity on every side. Precious stones give light to see people and by discernment we teach and counsel our fellows. The turrets of the fleur-de-lis have two branches spreading sideways, one to the right and the other to the left and the third going straight above the head. By the perfection of virtue, which is love, we spread out the two side branches of love; on the right side to our friends and on the left to our enemies. And there is a third going straight to God above the understanding, the head of the soul. This is the crown of life which, by grace, we may obtain here below *(Discernment of Stirrings)*.

Here the author gives full rein to a typically medieval love of symbolism. The crown he describes is similar to that worn by the kings of Scotland, France and England.

It was simple in structure so its component parts were all the more clear and stark. Gold signifies wisdom. The carefully pictured image shows that the infusion of love is closely bound up with the acquisition of wisdom. This is consonant with the teaching of St Thomas Aquinas. Although there is an 'intellectual' wisdom such as we should expect a professional person would give of his or her area of expertise, there is another sort of wisdom which has an affinity to love:

> (Wisdom is) a correct judgement made through rational investigation (and as such) is an intellectual virtue. But to judge aright through a certain fellowship with divine things, belongs to that wisdom which is a gift of the Holy Spirit ... So it belongs to wisdom first to contemplate the divine realities ... (and then direct human actions). *(Summa Theologiae II, II, 45, 2).*

Our author devoted a considerable portion of the *Privy Counsel* (chapters 3, 4 and 5) to commenting on certain sections of the book of *Proverbs*. The injunction 'worship God with your substance' (Prov 3:9) he takes as the complete self-offering involved in contemplative prayer. And then after that 'with your first fruits feed the poor' (Prov 3:9) we must give ourselves in the service of others:

> we are bound to foster and feed in this life, all who are our brothers and sisters either in the flesh or in grace; and we must do this by both physical and spiritual means *(Privy Counsel 3).*

This returns us to the central Christian mystery. We can offer ourselves to God and to others because of Jesus Christ. He has given himself for us:

> Christ's sacrifice was made for all men and not just for some individuals in particular. Thus he truly and perfectly sacrifices himself for the good of all. He does all that is possible to knit all men to God as effectively as he himself is *(Privy Counsel 3).*

This is the wisdom which is the power of God (1 Cor 1:24). Contemplative prayer is at the heart of this mystery and familiarity with it enables us to grow in wisdom.

And the crown is also adorned with discernment. This also issues from familiarity with God. Discernment enables us to 'teach and counsel' others. Often we look for rules-of-thumb and facile solutions when charged with the responsibility of guiding others. But there is no easy route to real discernment: it certainly is not merely the result of any training in the complexities of diplomacy or the intricacies of inter-personal relations. Long familiarity with God, and a growing knowledge of self, does something mysterious to the human being. So we do not study techniques so much as strive for fidelity:

> For silence is not God, and speaking is not God; fasting is not God and eating is not God; solitude is not God, and companionship is not God; nor indeed any other pair of such contraries.
>
> He is hid between them.
>
> He cannot be found by anything your soul does; but only by the love of your heart. He may not be known by reason; nor can he be thought, held or searched by understanding; but he can be loved and chosen by the true and loving desire of your heart. So choose him; and you are silent in your speaking, and speaking in your silence, fasting in your eating and eating in your fasting and so forth for the rest ...
>
> The very thing that you are experiencing will well know to tell you when you should speak and when to be silent *(Discernment of Stirrings)*.

Godliness will have pervaded the whole human being: God will be all in all (Rev).

20. Transfiguration

> *Regarding what they say about St Martin and St Stephen: although they saw such things with their bodily eyes, this was done by a miracle as a way of certifying spiritual truth. For they knew quite well that the cloak of St Martin was not literally on the body of Christ; for he had no need of it to keep him from the cold. The miraculous likeness was for all of us who can be saved and who are spiritually united to the body of Christ. Whosoever clothes a poor man and does any other good deed for the love of God (whether it be a spiritual or corporal kindness done to anyone in need) certainly does it to Christ. Such people shall be rewarded for it just as surely as if they had done it for Christ's own body. Christ himself says this in the gospel. Yet he thought that not sufficient, so he affirmed it by a miracle. For this reason he showed himself to St Martin by a miracle. The revelations that people have by way of bodily likeness in this life, have spiritual meaning. And I think if those to whom they were shown had been sufficiently spiritual, or could have conceived their spiritual significance, they would never have been shown them in bodily form. Therefore let us pick off the rough shell and eat the sweet kernel* (The Cloud 58).

Our author has no doubt that miraculous events take place. He merely alludes to the 'great wonders and signs' (Acts 6:8) performed by St Stephen; and then makes more explicit reference to the incident in the life of St Martin (d 397) in which, after giving his cloak to a poor man, he was shown a vision of Christ. These opening sentences display a cryptic style as though they formed a reply to a query posed by the young man for whom *The Cloud* was written. The clear import is that while stories of the miraculous can teach us spiritual truths, they are not to be merely an occasion for wonder and curiosity; let alone are they the essence of the Christian faith. Indeed he makes it abundantly clear that if our faith were strong enough we would have no need of miracles. This was sound advice for people who had a hankering after miraculous signs. And it still has some value today. Our author is much more concerned to relate contemplative prayer to the *ordinary* things of life. Prayer should enable us to obtain the grace to walk in the darkness of faith and to appreciate something of the deep significance latent in commonplace events. We are to get to the heart of the business of Christian living: 'pick off the rough shell, and eat the sweet kernel'. The same image is to be found in Walter Hilton:

> (When good deeds) become acts of charity, a person has a love of virtue. He has gnawed through and broken the bitter shell of the nut, and feeds on its kernel
> *(Ladder of Perfection I 14).*

This implies that a vigorous effort has been made to get to the heart of the Christian quest. Actions can be performed for very superficial reasons: perhaps simply because they 'have' to be done in some sense; or might be 'useful' to obtain some immediate goals; or they might merely be offering others the dry bones of 'good manners'. All these attitudes might have some use, but the Christian seeks to 'pick off (such a) rough shell'. Deeds done under the influence of the love of God take on their essential nature: we have 'gnawed through' to the kernel.

So this brings us to the heart or the 'kernel' of Christian living. Ordinary, simple and mundane actions can be performed with a freedom, generosity and courtesy that can only come from the love of God within our hearts. Contemplation empowers us to 'transfigure' the commonplace and the homely actions that make up our daily tasks. This is the great truth to which our author alludes when he says: 'Christ himself says so in the gospel'. The simple courtesies of life can have an immediate reference to Christ and so give us an opening, the way, into eternal life:

> I was hungry and you gave me food,
> I was thirsty and you gave me drink,
> I was a stranger and you welcomed me,
> I was naked and you clothed me,
> I was sick and you visited me,
> I was in prison and you came to me
> *(Mt 25:35-36)*.

And the faithful Christian, surprised at the implication of long forgotten actions asks 'When ...? When did I see you hungry, thirsty, estranged, naked, sick or imprisoned?' And the gospel words assert the powerful connection between the simple, kindly deed, the person of Christ, and the eternal reality of God's kingdom:

> As you did it to one of the least of these my brethren, you did it to me ... Come, O blessed of my Father, inherit the kingdom prepared for you *(Mt 25:40,34)*.

Many contemporary Christians are confronted with situations where the gospel words have an immediate and literal relevance and application. All of us must be in sympathy with such situations and hold them in our prayer. But it is also true that we all meet situations where people are hungry for the minimum of companionship; where people thirst for a kindly and encouraging word in the midst of their particular desert; almost every country in the world has some aliens and refugees; there are many who have been stripped naked of dignity and their right to a good name; and there are countless people imprisoned in fears and anxieties and addictions. The Christian man or woman of prayer is empowered to do something, however little it seems.

Small gestures do have a cosmic impact. The Christian who stands in the darkness of faith gains a deepening conviction of the potential of each small act, though its significance remains clouded and its appearance trivial.

Contemplative prayer does not lift one 'off the planet', nor does it prompt us to treat others with a detached and cold manner, or an overly serious 'religiosity'; nor does the presence of grace mean that the contemplative acts like a puppet on a string. The contemplative should be profoundly human and quietly humane. The mysterious nexus between the desert of prayer and the market place of activity is hidden in depths that people can hardly guess. There is, as it were, a perfect harmony between the great mystery of God on the one hand, and the human event on the other. Dietrich Bonhoeffer tried to capture something of this great truth when he wrote:

> God wants us to love him eternally with our whole hearts — not in such a way as to injure or weaken our earthly love, but to provide a kind of *cantus firmus* to which the other melodies of life provide the counterpoint ... Where the *cantus firmus* is clear and plain, the counterpoint can be developed to its limits. The two are 'undivided and yet distinct', in the words of the Chalcedonian Definition, like Christ in his divine and human natures. May not the attraction and importance of polyphony in music consist in its being a musical reflection of this Christological fact and therefore of our *vita christiana*?
> *(Letters and Papers from Prison pp 99-100).*

The 'cantus firmus', contemplative prayer, does not lessen one's humanity; but rather it deepens it and gives it a fuller meaning. The person committed to such prayer is still involved in all manner of duties and tasks, most of which pass quickly and are forgotten, and all of which probably seem so small. Yet they are a real presence of Christ in the world, and speak of things unseen and minister to others something of the beauty of God's love. But the contemplative is not merely increasingly convinced of the significance of the simple action; he or she is also increasingly human. Indeed there is no other 'atmosphere' in which our humanity can grow, but in God.

In his *Life of Antony* St Athanasius draws a picture of the saint after he had been living a life of great asceticism and prayer for nearly 20 years. He had been living as a hermit in a remote place, and now many wished to learn from his great wisdom:

> When they saw him, they wondered at the sight for he had the same habit of body as before, and was neither fat, like a man without exercise, nor lean from fasting and striving with demons, but he was just the same as they had known him before his retirement. And again his soul was free from blemish, for it was neither contracted as if by grief, nor relaxed by pleasure, nor possessed by laughter or dejection, for he was not troubled when he beheld the crowd, nor overjoyed at being saluted by so many. But he was altogether guided by reason, and abiding in a natural state *(Life of Antony 14)*.

Antony had been 'transfigured' into a 'whole' human being, a 'holy' man, one totally in tune with God and yet still genuinely himself. The process did not render him less human, rather it made him what he should be — an image and likeness of God. Athanasius then continued his narrative to relate something of Antony's care for those who sought his ministry. And this is the very point to which our author leads us:

> Whoever performs this work of contemplation will be totally influenced by it in body as well as in soul. Indeed it should make contemplatives very attractive to each man or woman who encounters them. So much so, indeed, that the least favoured man or woman alive who by grace comes to engage in this work will find that their appearance would be suddenly and graciously changed. Indeed every good person who met such a contemplative would be very glad and joyful to have their friendship. They would be convinced that by their company they were strengthened in spirit and helped in grace to come closer to God *(The Cloud 54).*

Here humanity has very simply become the vehicle of grace. Without any drama the person has a 'transfigured' humanity, one which shows forth in some measure, the beauty and the love of God. In several places in his writings our author speaks of grace influencing the human will; and that God himself teaches the work of contemplation. And here he speaks of the impact of grace on the whole person. Grace is not merely a mysterious presence that enlightens the mind, enlivens the heart and liberates the will: it is also evident in the body. This stands to reason: we know that such things as peace or pain, anger or joy, are in some way reflected in facial expressions. So too, the presence of God has an effect. This is very much in the tradition of the Eastern Fathers of the Church who speak of the 'deification' of the whole human being:

> In the same way in which the soul and the body are united, God should become accessible for participation by the soul and, through the soul's intermediary, by the body, in order that the soul might receive an unchanging character and the body immortality; and finally that the whole person should become God, deified by the grace of God-become-man, becoming whole man, soul and body, by nature; becoming whole God, soul and body, by grace *(St Maximus the Confessor, quoted in John Meyendorff, Byzantine Theology, p 164).*

Such teaching has its Christian roots in the epistle of St Peter where he speaks of our becoming 'partakers of the divine nature' (2 Pet 1:4). And the same Eastern tradition connects this with the Transfiguration of our Lord:

> Hear the words of the Apostle: 'Our bodies are the temples of the Holy Spirit' (1 Cor 6:19) and again, 'We are the house of God' (Heb 3:6) and God himself says 'I will dwell in them and will walk in them and I shall be their God' (2 Cor 6:16) ... Moreover, the transformation and transfiguration of our human nature, its deification and transfiguration — were ... accomplished by Christ from the start, from the moment in which he assumed our nature. Thus he was divine before, but he bestowed at the time of his Transfiguration a divine power upon the eyes of the apostles and enabled them to look up and see for themselves
> *(St Gregory Palamas, The Triads I and III).*

We are called, by our Christian baptism, to share in this mystery of human transfiguration. Clearly this transfiguration is not some superficial form of spiritual cosmetic nor a matter of techniques which enable people to win friends and influence people. It is something which touches the mysterious depths of the human being:

> Therefore seek this gift, whoever by grace may do so. If you truly possess it, you will well know how to govern yourself, and all your possessions, by its strength. If the need should arise you will be able to discern well all manner of human types and dispositions. You would have the facility of making yourself loved by all who lived with you, whether they were habitual sinners or not, without sinning yourself. You would be a cause of wonder to all who saw you, and you would draw others, by the help of grace, to the same spiritual work that you practice
> *(The Cloud 54).*

The picture he draws is of a human being with strength of character; an independent self-possession that is not enslaved to things; one who is able to judge others with wisdom; at ease with others and able to put them at ease also; and, although fragile, such a person has convictions that are not readily and easily jettisoned when under pressure from surrounding attitudes.

The most powerful gospel witness is a life lived without affectation, apology or pugnacity. In a sermon entitled 'Profession without Ostentation' John Henry Newman remarked:

> consider how great a profession and yet a profession how unconscious and modest, arises from the mere ordinary manner in which any strict Christian lives. Let this thought be a satisfaction to uneasy minds which fear lest they are not confessing Christ, yet dread to display. Your *life* displays Christ without your intending it. You cannot help it. Your *words and deeds* will show on the long run, where your treasure is, and your heart
> *(Parochial and Plain Sermons I, 155).*

Rather different is the contrast the author draws between such witness and the shallow and superficial posturing of those who seek to impress:

> The contemplative's countenance and words are full of real wisdom and also full of fervour and fruitful; they are spoken in a sober gentleness without any falsehood. Such is far removed from the posturing and pretence of hypocrites. For there are some who employ all their resources of personality to study how they might bolster themselves by their words. They seek to prop up themselves on every side by meek pious words and devout gestures. They are more concerned to appear good in the sight of others than to be truly so in the sight of God and his angels. Such folk attach great importance to expressing sorrow for some unintentional gesture or

> unseemly or unfitting word spoken before their fellows; but on the other hand they will have very little sorrow for a thousand vile thoughts and stinking sinful movements willfully and recklessly committed in the sight of God and the saints and angels in heaven *(The Cloud 54)*.

Harsh words these. They remind us of our ambivalence. They also recall our abiding need for mercy so that we genuinely seek God and not just use fine words about him; or merely seek an impressive appearance, without a heart genuinely possessed by him. These words remind us of the Lord's injunction:

> Woe to you, scribes and Pharisees, hypocrites! for you cleanse the outside of the cup, and of the plate, but inside they are full of extortion and rapacity. You blind Pharisees! first cleanse the inside of the cup and the plate, that the outside may also be clean *(Mt 23:25-26)*.

We humans are always in danger of some duplicity: the work of healing and transformation lasts a lifetime. As we seek to love the mystery of transfiguration we would do well to keep in mind the insight of the great artist Raphael. His portrayal of the transfiguration also included the story of the cure of the epileptic boy (Mk 9:14-29). The painting is divided into two sections. The upper portion depicts the scene on the mountain top; it is a source of light which floods over the people in the lower section of the painting. This latter part depicts a world of confusion and pain; a world in need of healing. Some figures point expectantly to Christ; others seem engrossed in the world's pain and burdened by it; others again seem strangely detached. But *this* is the world that needs the light of the transfigured Christ; and we are part of this world, as well as being instruments of transformation.

How shall the task be done? Probably not by any dramatic gestures on our part; but rather by allowing the grace of prayer to touch the everyday event. After the struggle up the mountain top, the exciting revelation of the glory of Christ, their involvement in the cloud of mystery, the disciples 'lifted their eyes and saw no one but Jesus only' (Mt 17:8). We too must seek to come from prayer and see 'no one but Jesus only': Jesus in the hungry, thirsty, estranged, naked, sick and imprisoned. They might not always seem attractive; and indeed they might all too rarely be grateful. Which reminds us that we must see Christ in ourselves, transfiguring the world through our dealings with others — if we but allow him to do so. We and they are in 'travail until Christ be formed' in us (Gal 4:19).

★ ★ ★

In his rather rambling approach our author has brought us into contact with all the great aspects of contemplative prayer. Such prayer involves a deep personal commitment to Christ and his mission; and this grows within the body of Christ, the Church. This is the place where Christ gives us his healing touch, nourishes us on his transfigured body in the Eucharist and brings us into a loving relationship with the Father. Yet all this is a mystery; it grows in a time and place of darkness where we see nothing and feel little. Yet the darkness is a creative, healing and loving one; it is making something of us. We are increasingly involved in the great work of God in the world.

But we must be prepared to give God the time and place of prayer. It is all too easy to talk *about* it; it is rather more difficult to *do* it! In a moment of gentle humour de Caussade remarked:

> If we wish to quench our thirst, we must lay aside books which explain thirst and take a drink
> *(Self Abandonment p 38).*

And our author gives us a gentle prompt: contemplation is something that cannot be described, it can only be experienced. So we should actually *pray*, and *do* this *work* of contemplation because:

> Everything that is said about it is not the thing itself, but is only *about* it *(Privy Counsel 7)*.

Books of general Christian interest as well as books on theology, scripture, spirituality and mysticism are published by Burns and Oates Limited.
A free catalogue will be sent on request:
BURNS AND OATES Dept A,
Wellwood, North Farm Road, Tunbridge Wells,
Kent TN2 3DR